Feasting on the Word®

CHILDREN'S SERMONS
FOR YEAR B

D1570212

Also available in this series

Feasting on the Word® Children's Sermons for Year C
Feasting on the Word® Children's Sermons for Year A

Feasting on the Word®

CHILDREN'S SERMONS
FOR YEAR B

Carol A. Wehrheim

WESTMINSTER
JOHN KNOX PRESS
LOUISVILLE · KENTUCKY

First edition
Published by Westminster John Knox Press
Louisville, Kentucky

17 18 19 20 21 22 23 24 25 26—10 9 8 7 6 5 4 3 2 1

All Scripture stories and poetry in quotation marks are paraphrased from New Revised Standard Version of the Bible (NRSV), copyright © 1989, and the Common English Bible (CEB), copyright © 2011.

Book design by Drew Stevens
Cover design by Lisa Buckley Design and Allison Taylor

Library of Congress Cataloging-in-Publication Data
Names: Wehrheim, Carol A., author.
Title: Feasting on the word : children's sermons for Year B / Carol A.
  Wehrheim.
Description: Louisville, KY : Westminster John Knox Press, 2017. | Includes
  index. |
Identifiers: LCCN 2017006343 (print) | LCCN 2017029757 (ebook) | ISBN
  9781611648188 (ebk.) | ISBN 9780664261085 (pbk. : alk. paper)
Subjects: LCSH: Children's sermons. | Common lectionary (1992). Year B. |
  Church year sermons--Juvenile literature. | Preaching to children.
Classification: LCC BV4315 (ebook) | LCC BV4315 .W355 2017 (print) | DDC
  252/.53--dc23
LC record available at https://lccn.loc.gov/2017006343

♾ The paper used in this publication meets the minimum requirements of the American National Standard for Information Sciences—Permanence of Paper for Printed Library Materials, ANSI Z39.48-1992.

Most Westminster John Knox Press books are available at special quantity discounts when purchased in bulk by corporations, organizations, and special-interest groups. For more information, please e-mail SpecialSales@wjkbooks.com.

*For all the children who have listened to my stories
and helped me polish my storytelling gifts*

Contents

LENT

EASTER

*During Ordinary Time, or the season after Pentecost, the lectionary offers two streams, or tracks, of readings: the semicontinuous and complementary streams of the Revised Common Lectionary. See page xvii of the introduction for more information.

Acknowledgments

A number of years ago, I saw a notice of a storytelling workshop to be held on the Princeton University campus. It was a weeklong seminar led by Susan Danoff. I didn't know Susan, but I wanted to know more about storytelling in the hope that I, a curriculum writer and editor, could find ways to write more engaging Bible stories for children. What I discovered in Susan was not only a spellbinding storyteller but an excellent educator. I have described that week as the best week of continuing education I have experienced. From that seminar I not only learned how to tell a story but also discovered the power of story. Since then, I have come to believe with more and more certainty that the church must regain its storytelling history, so that we tell the story to one another, face to face.

Many of the stories here are based on stories in the *Feasting on the Word* curriculum. Although I have written or revised them all, I have often been helped by a turn of phrase or point of view that was drawn from one of the writers for this series. I am especially indebted to Sharon Harding, who wrote many of the summer sessions and who gave me lovely words to begin as I wrote the Bible stories to tell to the congregation. Without the suggestion from David Maxwell that this book would be helpful to congregations, these stories would not be written down for others to tell.

There are few things I would rather do than tell Bible stories to children in church school or vacation Bible school or to the congregation in worship. I hope you will discover what joy can be found in giving these stories to others, whatever the age, and how it enriches the depth of your Bible study and faith.

Introduction

The Importance of Stories

"Children, come join me for the story," the storyteller beckoned, with arms open. Girls and boys hurried forward to get a spot next to a friend. Some children hesitated, holding a parent's hand, as they walked slowly to the front of the sanctuary. When everyone was settled, the storyteller began, "Long, long ago, even before Jesus was born . . ." You could feel the congregation, adults and children, relax and settle in to hear the story. A good story, told well, has something for everyone, from age four to ninety-four and beyond. Certainly the Bible is filled with good stories. And worship is an occasion for all generations to hear the story together. Hearing the story together is no small thing, for we Christians are a storied people, and hearing it at the same time and in the same space brings all generations together.

Many reasons are given for including a children's sermon or time with the children in the order of worship. At one end of the spectrum, it functions as a way to transition the children from the worship service to their church school classes. In that case, the little talk or story may have nothing to do with anything else that takes place in worship or in what children do in their church school classes. Too often, it is a story or talk that is prepared hurriedly and ends with a moral, one that is often beyond the understanding of the children.

But let's back up for a moment. Why is storytelling of any kind important? Stories—family stories, community stories, national stories, faith stories—are how we pass values from one generation to the next. These stories tell us who we are and what is important to our families, our tribes, our nations, our faith communities. These stories bind us together. In this same way, Bible stories bind us together as the people of God. They tell us who we are and whose we are. They help us see God at work in our world. They incorporate us into the body of Christ. And stories begin to work this wonder when we are very, very young. What better time, then, to tell Bible stories on a regular basis than when the faith community is gathered in its most unique and faithful act, the worship of God.

When the Bible story that is told matches the sermon text, the story provides an entry point into the sermon for adults and children as they ponder the story and how it is proclaimed in the sermon. Repetition of the story as it is told and as it is read from the Bible reinforces the text, its structure and plot, and need not be a concern for worship planners.

When that text is also the passage studied in church school, whether for children or all ages—which is possible when using a lectionary-based curriculum such as *Feasting on the Word*—the possibilities for faith formation are multiplied. But these optimal conditions are not necessary to nurture faith through telling Bible stories in worship.

The ultimate goal is to tell the Bible story so the listeners' imaginations and hearts catch fire, as happened to the disciples on the road to Emmaus when Jesus told the stories of the prophets. Bible stories help us recognize Jesus and meet the God who sent him to us.

Another reason for telling Bible stories in worship is to free these stories from the page. When Moses spoke to "all Israel" as the people were about to enter the promised land without him, he told them that everyone was responsible for teaching the children, and this was no small thing "but their very life." Every adult in the church has some responsibility for telling the story to the next generation. Indeed, the congregation promises that to each infant baptized. When the story is told in worship, adults have a model to follow. They find that it's just fine to laugh at a humorous detail or to wonder what happened next. They also learn that they don't have to include every word or get everything right. After all, this is how Bible stories were passed from generation to generation, by word of mouth from one person to the next. Not every adult will tell the story to the congregation but might tell it to one or two children or grandchildren.

Everyone is a storyteller. Think about it. When you find a bargain at the mall and phone a friend to tell about it, you are telling a story. When a child asks, "What was school like when you were in second grade, Grandmom?" and you tell about your second grade classroom, you are telling a story. Stories help us know each other, our dreams, our fears, and our joys. We may not all be comfortable telling stories before a group, whether children or adults, but we are all storytellers, and some of us are called to be storytellers of the church's story to the congregation, the whole congregation.

One more thought about telling Bible stories in the service of worship. If you have heard StoryCorps on a public broadcasting station, you know that personal stories can delight, enlighten, heal, and bridge gaps in relationships. David Isay, the originator of StoryCorps, describes the stories collected as conversations in sacred space.[1] No, they are not recorded in a religious building, but the stories are the meeting of two souls with a facilitator, whose task is to listen, listen intently, to bear witness to the story and storyteller. Perhaps the adults in the congregation are the silent witnesses to the story when it is told in worship. If that is the case, adults are included in the audience for the story. It's not for children only.

For all of these reasons about the importance of story and the place Bible stories have in nurturing the faith in all ages, perhaps we ought to think of the time when children come forward as a time to tell the Bible story in worship rather than a children's sermon or time with the children. The story is for everyone present; it's just that the children get a front row seat. It's a story, not a sermon. Thinking of this worship element as a children's sermon has fostered too many pious talks that end with a moral. Or children are subjected to an object lesson before they are able to comprehend metaphor, and they become fixated on the object. Occasionally something said leading up to the story distracts children from even hearing the story. Many years ago, a person giving the children's sermon began by telling the children that he had hit a deer on the way to church. A mother reported later that her boys could talk about nothing else the rest of the day. Did they hear the message of the children's sermon? Probably not. Tell the story. Tell it with all the enthusiasm and delight that you can muster so that God's Word is given to each person in the sanctuary.

1. David Isay, "Transcript for David Isay—Listening as an Act of Love," *On Being*, April 17, 2014, http://www.onbeing.org/program/dave-isay-the-everyday-art-of-listening /transcript/6274.

Preparing the Story

This book provides a story for telling in worship based on one of the Year B lectionary texts for each Sunday, from the first Sunday in Advent to Reign of Christ/Christ the King Sunday (the end of the church year), as well as a story for Christmas. Also included are four stories for special times in the congregation's life. These stories are about five minutes long.

To prepare to tell a story provided here, read both the story and text that is the basis for the story. Adapt the story so the style and the words or phrases are comfortable for you. Don't try to memorize it word for word. You are *telling* the story, not reciting it.

Practice telling the story over and over. Tell it to a mirror, to your pet, to anyone who will listen. As you tell it again and again, you will find phrases and word combinations that are natural for you, but keep the language simple and appropriate for children. Then it is appropriate for those adults who are listening intently too. Using language and concepts the children will understand doesn't make it boring for youth and adults. A story told with enthusiasm will draw in the entire congregation.

As you practice telling the story, notice how your arms or head move naturally to the emotions or content of the story. Perhaps you stand tall and strong to emphasize the power of Jesus when he calms the storm. Or you might shield your eyes and look into the distance as you tell about the lost sheep. If you find motions difficult, pantomime the story, using actions and no words. You may discover some natural movements in the process.

With a longer story, you may find it helpful to get the scenes firmly in your mind. One method is to outline the story and remember the outline by memorizing the opening words for each scene.

Have the opening and closing sentences firmly in mind. This is an exception to telling, not memorizing the story. Knowing how you will begin and end relieves some of the stress. Being prepared with a strong concluding sentence will keep the story from drifting away from you and the listeners.

When telling the Bible story, sound practice suggests that you do not ask a question of the children. Someone will answer you, and more often than not the answer provokes a chuckle from the congregation. Too many children have been hurt by that ripple of laughter, because they answer with all seriousness. The better road is to avoid asking questions.

Occasionally, a child will ask a question in the middle of the story. For example, a girl of about seven asked, "What does 'getting even' mean?" The story was about the rules from God in Leviticus 19, and the storyteller said, "When someone is mean to you, don't try to get even." The storyteller, in a sentence, explained "getting even." The child responded, "Oh, I thought maybe it was getting everything right." One can understand why a child might think that. Such distractions and other kinds will happen. Take them in stride and try to keep your focus.

Telling the Story to the Whole Congregation

Everyone comes along when a story is told well. And most people, with practice, can learn to tell a story well. Here are some things to consider:

Stand facing the congregation with the children facing you. Sitting in the congregation and listening to a disembodied story, when you know the storyteller is using motions and movement, is distracting. Encourage the children to look at you by saying something like, "Sit so I can see your eyes."

Look at the children and focus on one child who is eagerly waiting to hear the story for a moment. Then begin with the opening sentence you carefully crafted.

When the story includes a quoted section from the Bible, as in a letter from the New Testament, write or type the quote. Roll it up like a scroll and open it to read during the story. Or place your paraphrase in the Bible and open it to read the paraphrase. Use a Bible that the children will recognize so they know that what you are reading is from this very book.

While motions and movement can contribute to the excitement and action of the story, try to keep your own actions to a well-selected minimum. Too much movement is distracting from the story. Constant pacing back and forth makes the listeners dizzy.

At the end of the story, after you have said that carefully prepared closing sentence, hold the gaze of a child who has been listening intently for just a moment before praying.

Enjoy telling the story. What a wonderful gift you are giving to each person who is listening, whether this is the first time a child has heard it or the adults know it backwards and forwards. But that's the wonderful thing, the story you tell may invite adults familiar with it to look at the words from another angle. The wondrous thing about the Bible is that there is always more to say and ponder.

Writing Other Bible Stories to Tell to the Congregation

Sometimes the lectionary texts aren't what you want or the sermon text is not from the lectionary. Then the storyteller is responsible for writing a story. The story "Queen Vashti" (pp. xxv–xxvi) was written for that reason, since Esther 1 never appears in the Revised Common Lectionary. Once the text is chosen, follow these steps.

1. Read at least one commentary on the passage. Look for interpretations or information that will guide how you approach the story. For example, if the story text is from Philippians, explain that Paul wrote this letter to the church in Philippi while he was in prison. For the story of Queen Vashti, notice how the story begins because it is difficult to date the book of Esther and because it was certainly written long after the events it records.

2. Read the text in several translations, including one with a limited English vocabulary (CEV or Good News). Notice how the translations differ and where they are alike or similar. If you are the preacher and the storyteller, steps one and two will serve for the sermon preparation and the story preparation. The other steps may also help you move into the story as you begin your sermon preparation. Be open to the possibility.

3. Tell the story to yourself. If you aren't sure of the sequence, just keep going. This will help you establish a rhythm for the story and identify the parts of it that are important and memorable. Go back to the text and see what you missed or added.

4. Write the story as you would like to tell it. One of the

most difficult things about writing the story is selecting words that convey meaning to the children. Bible stories are not occasions to show off your vocabulary or clever phrasing, for the children or the adults. Paraphrase sections of speeches or letters you want to include. This is a rough draft. Pay no attention to grammatical details, misspelled words, or sentence structure.

5. Compare your written story to the text. Add missing details that are important to the story. Are there details that will enliven the storytelling that you can add without compromising the text? Check on the sequence of events. Is your story faithful to the text and what you know about it from reading the commentary? If you compare "Queen Vashti" to Esther 1, you will soon notice details that are not part of the story, such as the names of the king's eunuchs and the details about the drinking party. Yet the essence of the story and Vashti's role in setting up the necessity for a new queen come through clearly.

Generally, you can omit details that are inappropriate for children without damaging the intent of the story. For example, in Year B, the Gospel lectionary text for Proper 20 is Mark 9:30–37. Verses 30–32 are Jesus' prediction of his death, while verses 33–37 tell of Jesus' conversation with the disciples about who is the greatest. When preparing the story for telling in worship, base the story on verses 33–37. Omitting the first three verses doesn't change the story about when Jesus and the disciples reach Capernaum. When you look at that text carefully, it is two stories. As a rule of thumb, keep to one story for this moment in worship.

6. The opening and closing sentences of the story are especially important. Write the opening sentence carefully

to get the attention of the listeners right away. Look at "Queen Vashti" and notice how the opening sentence tells the listeners that this is a story from the Old Testament, a story that Jesus may have heard as a child. The words "A very long time ago, way, way longer than anyone here can remember" draws listeners in to hear how the story unfolds. The closing sentence is just as important because this may help the listeners remember the story and helps you draw the story to a close. This is not a moral or explanation of the story; it is the conclusion of the story. Look at "Queen Vashti." The closing sentence encourages the listeners to ponder the story on their own and clearly marks that this is the end of Vashti's story. Indeed, nothing more is said about her in the book of Esther. If you read Esther 1, Vashti's story doesn't have an ending. The closing sentence of the story doesn't provide an ending either, but it does provide a way to end the story being told.

7. Now you are ready to rehearse. As suggested earlier, rehearsal of the story will make all the difference in your role as storyteller. Tell the story aloud often. Let your body move naturally to the story's emotions and content. If you find motions difficult, try pantomiming the story, or if you enjoy drawing, sketch the story in scenes. You may discover some natural movements in the process. Examine vocabulary and figures of speech to be sure you haven't strayed from language accessible to children. And memorize the opening and closing sentences so you have them firmly in mind. Incorporate them into the story so they sound natural.

Queen Vashti

A very long time ago, way, way longer than anyone here can remember, King Asheruerus ruled over all the land from Ethiopia to India. He wanted to show all the important men of those countries just how rich and important he was, so he had a big feast, a banquet. He invited the councilors of the court, the generals of the army, and the governors of the lands. This feast was not just for one night, or two or three nights, or even ten nights. It went on for 180 nights.

When that big party ended, the king had another party just for the men of Susa where his royal palace was. He held it in the courtyard of the palace. The courtyard had big marble pillars. They were draped with fine blue cloth, held in place with silver rings. The floor sparkled with mother-of-pearl and beautiful colored stones.

While the king was entertaining the men, Queen Vashti had a party for the women. It was in another part of the palace. I think they were far enough apart that one party didn't bother the other one.

On the seventh night of his party, the king was feeling pretty good and very important. He sent seven servants with a message for Queen Vashti.

The servants said to Queen Vashti, "A message from the king. 'Come to me. Wear your royal crown so all the men of Susa will see what a beautiful queen I have.'"

Queen Vashti thought for a moment. It was dangerous not to obey the king's command, but she was entertaining her own guests. She sent this message back to the king: "I will not come."

Was the king angry when he got her message! The more he thought about it, the angrier he got. "What must be done with Queen Vashti?" he asked the seven councilors of the court. They huddled together and whispered. "If the queen does not obey the king, our wives will find out and they won't pay any attention to us. We cannot have that!" So they said to the king, "Send a royal decree to all the land. Say that because Queen Vashti did not obey your command to come to you, she is never able to come to you again; and get a new queen."

The king smiled. He liked that idea. In fact, the more he thought about it, the more he liked it. So a decree went out to all the land, from India to Ethiopia: "Because Queen Vashti refused to obey the king, she can never come before him again."

Now some people feel sorry for Vashti, but I think she was a brave and intelligent woman. Although she was no longer queen, she still lived in the palace, and I think she rather liked it that way.

A Word about the Lectionary

During Ordinary Time, or the season after Pentecost, the Revised Common Lectionary offers two streams, or tracks, in the readings: semicontinuous and complementary streams. Each stream uses the same Epistle and Gospel reading, but the Old Testament and Psalms lections are different. The semicontinuous track allows congregations to read continually through a book of Scripture from week to week. In the complementary track, the Old Testament readings are chosen to relate to (or complement) the Gospel reading of the day. In both cases, the psalm is understood as a response to the Old Testament reading. This book provides a story for each week during Ordinary Time, no matter which track a church uses. Many weeks include a story from each track.

Since the numbering of the Sundays after Pentecost varies from year to year, the designation of "Proper" is used here, as it is in the *Feasting on the Word* commentaries and Worship Companions. It can be confusing to navigate the various ways churches designate Sundays; a handy resource for viewing all those labels in one place can be found at http://lectionary.library.vanderbilt.edu/, a user-friendly site provided to the public by Vanderbilt University.

❧ LECTIONARY DATES ❧

Lament and Joy
Isaiah 64:1–9

Long, long ago the people of Israel wondered whether God had forgotten them. They had been captured by the Babylonian army and taken back to Babylon to live. They didn't want to be there. They wanted to go back to their own land, in Jerusalem. But they had no choice. Now they had lived in Babylon for a long time. The prophet Isaiah knew what the people were thinking and feeling. He spoke to God for them:

> "God, if you would only come down from
>   the heavens,
>   the mountains would shake.
> "God, if you would speak to your enemies,
>   they would tremble before you.
> "But we have not heard from you;
>   you have not acted to help us."

Not only did the people think God had forgotten them; they were afraid that God was angry with them. Isaiah spoke for them again:

"Have you forgotten us because we have
    done wrong?
"No one calls on your name. We have
    forgotten you."

But Isaiah also remembered how God kept the promise with God's people. Isaiah remembered their close connection to God. He reminded the people, saying:

"God, we are clay,
    and you mold us like a potter.
"Each one of us is the work of your hands.
    Look at us now!"

Isaiah had many more words for the people, but none were more important than reminding them that they belonged to God no matter what and that God was their God, no matter what. As we begin the season of Advent, we want to remember these words and that we belong to God and that God is our God, no matter what.

Prayer: God, our God, open our eyes and our ears to recognize your presence in our lives and in the world. Amen.

A New Prophet in Town
Mark 1:1–8

From the prophet Isaiah in the Old Testament on the first Sunday of Advent, we go to the Gospel of Mark in the New Testament. Mark uses the words of Isaiah and other prophets to announce a new prophet for God, many, many years after Isaiah. This prophet also told about the one sent from God.

"Watch around you, for I, God, am sending my
        messenger to you.
"This messenger will get you ready.
"He will shout in the desert:
    'Get the road ready for God;
    make the path straight.'"

Then Mark told about this messenger of God, a man called John the baptizer. This John was quite different from everyone else around him. He wore clothes made from camel's hair, with a leather belt. He ate locusts and wild honey. He spent his days along the Jordan River.

John preached to the people that God wanted them to change their way of living. If they did this, God would forgive them all the things they did wrong. Then John baptized them.

People came from Jerusalem and all over Judea to hear John preach and to be baptized by him. It was quite amazing.

Some people wondered if John were the one God promised to send to them. "Not me," said John, "that one will be stronger than I am. I'm not good enough to untie the sandals of the one God promised to send."

John pointed to the river. "I baptize with water," he said, "but the one God promised to send will baptize with the Holy Spirit."

So the people waited some more for the one God promised to send, just as we wait during Advent.

Prayer: God of John and Isaiah, be with us as we wait for the one you promised to send. As we wait, help us prepare the way. Amen.

Turned Upside-down
Isaiah 61:1–4, 8–11

The book of Isaiah in the Old Testament is the longest book of the prophets. The messages from God came over many years. You heard some of those messages on the first Sunday of Advent. Now, on the third Sunday of Advent, we return to Isaiah. The messages in these chapters are also about the loneliness of God's people and their fear that God has forgotten them.

Isaiah has words of comfort and hope for the people. He tells them that all their troubles will be turned upside down. God's way of love and fairness will come to them. Then Isaiah tells the people:

"God's spirit is with me.
"God has sent me
   to tell good news to poor people,
   to care for people who are so sad,
   to tell people who feel like they are trapped that
     they are free,
   to tell people in prison that they will get out."

These words gave many people hope, but the prophet wasn't finished.

"I proclaim all this for God:
    to comfort people when someone has died,
    to say words of praise instead of discouragement."

These words were certainly good news to Israelites long ago. They wanted things to turn upside down soon, but they had to wait for God's time.

That time came when Jesus began his ministry. He announced what he would do by reading these words from Isaiah in the synagogue in his hometown of Nazareth. It was many, many years later, but God was still with the people.

Prayer: God of promises and good news, when we are sad or unhappy or feel like we are no good, let us remember these words. Then we will give you thanks for keeping promises. Amen.

A Special Task for a Simple Woman
Luke 1:26–38

Long, long after Isaiah gave good news and hope to the Israelites, but before John the baptizer called people to get ready for the one God would send, God sent Gabriel, a messenger of God, an angel, to get the mother of Jesus ready.

Mary was a poor young woman who lived in the village Nazareth. She was engaged to Joseph, a carpenter. She probably expected to live in Nazareth all her life and to raise her children there, close to her family and Joseph's family. Her life wasn't as quiet as she thought it was going to be.

Before she and Joseph were married, Mary was tending to her daily chores. Maybe she was grinding grain to bake bread or weeding the garden, but it probably wasn't anything special. Then, out of the nowhere, the angel Gabriel, a messenger from God, appeared right in front of her.

"Good news, Mary, God has chosen you," said Gabriel.

Mary looked at this person she had never seen in Nazareth. Who was he? What did he want? Where did he come from? What was going on?

"Mary, don't be afraid," he continued. "God has a special plan for you. You will have a baby boy, and you will name your baby Jesus."

That didn't help Mary very much. She was still confused. But Gabriel wasn't finished, "Your son will be great. He will be called 'Son of the Most High.' One day he will sit on the throne of David. He will rule forever."

Mary was astonished at these words. When she was finally able to speak, she said, "How can this happen? Joseph and I have not married."

Gabriel had an answer. "Your cousin Elizabeth is too old to have a baby, but she and Zechariah will also have a son in three months. The Holy Spirit will come over you. God can do anything, anything! Nothing is impossible for God."

Hearing all this, Mary said, "I am God's servant. I will have this baby boy, and I will name him Jesus."

As soon as she said this, Gabriel left, just as quickly as he had come.

Prayer: Surprising God, may we follow Mary's example and listen carefully for all that you want us to do. Amen.

They Named Him Jesus
Luke 2:1–20

Clippity clop went the donkey. Mary and Joseph were on the way to Bethlehem. It was not easy traveling when you were expecting a baby any day. But Joseph had to go there to register on the tax roll because he was of the family of David.

The sun was low in the sky, and Joseph was worried. He wanted to get his pregnant wife settled for the night as soon as possible. In Bethlehem, he looked for a room but not one was available. Finally, he settled for some space where the animals stayed. At least it was inside and quiet.

That very night Mary had her baby. She wrapped him tightly in cloths and laid him in the manger where the straw was put for the animals to eat. In a few days, she would name him Jesus.

In the fields outside Bethlehem, shepherds were watching over their sheep. Suddenly an angel of God was shining brightly in front of them. The bright light frightened the shepherds.

"Don't be afraid," said the angel. "I have joyful good news for you. Tonight, in Bethlehem, a baby was born. This baby is Christ the Lord. Go into the town and look for a baby, wrapped tightly in cloths, lying in a manger."

Before they could move, a great number of angels appeared in the sky. Their voices filled the air as they said, "Glory to God! On earth be peace among everyone whom God favors."

When the angels left, the shepherds went into Bethlehem. They soon found the baby, wrapped tightly in cloths, lying in a manger. They knelt down before the baby with his parents. They told them about the angels and their message. Everyone was amazed. Mary listened carefully to the shepherds and remembered what they said.

As the shepherds returned to their sheep, they praised God for everything they had seen and heard.

Prayer: God of wonder, we praise you as the shepherds did. We marvel at the wonderful news of the birth of Jesus, the Christ, our Lord and Savior. Amen.

Simeon and Anna
Luke 2:22–40

With the baby Jesus sound asleep in her arms, Mary and Joseph were on the way to Jerusalem. Obeying God's laws, they were going to present baby Jesus to God in the temple. Because they were not rich, they brought two turtle-doves, or young pigeons, as their gift to God.

Simeon, a faithful man, was in Jerusalem that day, and God's Spirit encouraged him to go to the temple. Simeon was eager for the one sent from God to come, and he prayed that this would happen while he was still alive. He believed that the Holy Spirit told him that he would see this special one.

So Simeon was in the temple when Mary and Joseph brought Jesus there. Simeon went to them and took Jesus from them to hold him. Then he said:

> "Now, God, I have seen what I longed to see;
>   I have seen your savior.
> "This child will be a light to all people everywhere,
>   and will be a glory to Israel."

Mary and Joseph looked at Simeon. What could he mean? Then Simeon blessed the parents. He looked right at Mary and said, "This child will see bad and good in Israel. Your heart will be broken."

Also in the temple was Anna, the daughter of the prophet Phanuel. She was eighty-four years old and had lived in the temple, worshiping God day and night, since her husband died many years ago.

She immediately came to Mary and Joseph. She saw the baby and began to praise God. She told everyone in the temple about this special baby Jesus.

On the way home to Nazareth, Mary and Joseph surely talked about what had happened in the temple that day. I wonder what they said.

Prayer: God, Simeon and Anna knew how special Jesus was as soon as they saw him. May we discover how special he is today too. Amen.

An Ancient Hymn
John 1:(1–9) 10–18

The gospel writer John was looking for a new way to tell the story of Jesus. As he thought, he realized he was humming a hymn that followers of Jesus sang together. The hymn talked about Jesus being with God from the very beginning.

Then John remembered another John, John the baptizer, and he wrote about him. "John the baptizer," he wrote, "was sent by God to tell people about Jesus, this light to the world."

Then it was back to the hymn with its words about how some people didn't welcome Jesus when he came and didn't see his light. But many people did, and they became his followers. They saw that he was a light from God.

Then John wrote more about John the baptizer, who said, "The one who comes after me will be greater than me."

The end of the hymn follows, reminding us that although we haven't seen God, the stories about Jesus, God's Son, show us who God is.

And that's the good news for us: We can't see God, but the gospel writers wrote down what Jesus said and did, and their stories show us who God is and teach us that God loves us. Good news!

Prayer: Amazing God, we thank you for Jesus' life and teachings because they teach us about you and your love. We want to tell others about Jesus and your love too. Amen.

Strangers at the Palace
Matthew 2:1–12

The people in King Herod's palace whispered, "Who do you think these travelers from the East are? Do you think they are trouble?" King Herod wondered the same thing. He didn't like strangers entering his territory.

These travelers, known as the magi, were smart. The first place they went in Jerusalem was to the palace of King Herod. They wanted to let him know that they came in peace. But they also had a question for him. "Where is the baby who is born king of the Jews?" they asked.

Their question surprised King Herod. He ruled over the Jews, and he didn't know anything about a baby who would be king. But he didn't let his guests know and gathered his advisors together to ask them about this baby king. They read the scrolls of the prophets and found a place where it said, "Bethlehem of Judah."

The king returned to his visitors and told them what the advisors said. Then he smiled and said to the travelers, "When you find this baby king, return to the palace and tell me so I can visit him too."

The magi left, and they continued to follow the star that had led them to Jerusalem. When they arrived in Bethlehem, they found Mary and her son Jesus in a house there. Right away, they dropped to their knees to worship the baby. Then they gave him gifts of gold, frankincense that smelled sweet when it was burned, and an expensive perfume called myrrh.

But they did not return to Jerusalem to tell the king where Jesus was. Before they left Bethlehem, they had a dream. In that dream, they were told not to go back to King Herod. So the magi returned to their homes, and they did not go anywhere near Jerusalem.

Prayer: God of wonder, God of light, you watched over the child Jesus, and you watch over us. Amen.

Mark's First Story about Jesus
Mark 1:4–11

In the Gospel of Mark, the first story about Jesus is his baptism. We meet John the baptizer first and learn that he lives in the wilderness and wears camel's hair clothes. John preaches by the Jordan River and tells people to turn their lives back to God and be baptized. He also announces, "Someone stronger than me will come from God. I baptize you with water from this river. That one will baptize you with the Holy Spirit."

On this day, John was preaching and baptizing at the Jordan River just like any other day. People on the bank of the river listened to him, and some decided to be baptized. But on this day, Jesus came from Nazareth to the Jordan River where John the baptizer was. John baptized him, dipping Jesus down into the water. As Jesus came up out of the water, he could see the clouds opening in the sky. Then the Holy Spirit, looking like a dove, came down to him.

From high in the sky, a voice said to Jesus, "My son, I love you very much. You make me very happy."

Mark ends the story of Jesus' baptism with these words. I wonder how Jesus felt. I wonder what John the baptizer thought.

Prayer: Dear God, thank you for loving us, your children, as you loved Jesus. In Jesus' name, we pray. Amen.

Samuel, Samuel
*1 Samuel 3:1–10 (11–20)**

The boy Samuel lived with Eli the priest in the temple. One day Eli, who was old and could barely see, was resting in his room. Samuel was lying down in the temple.

"Samuel," called a voice that Samuel thought was Eli. So he went to Eli and said, "I'm right here."

"I didn't call you," said Eli.

So Samuel went back and lay down. Again, the voice said, "Samuel." Again Samuel hurried to Eli, and Eli said, "I didn't call you. Go lie down."

Once more, the voice called, "Samuel." Samuel got up and went to Eli. Now Eli knew that it was God calling Samuel. He said, "I didn't call you. But if you hear the voice again, say, 'Speak, God. Samuel, your servant, is listening.'"

Samuel went back and waited. Sure enough, in a few minutes, the voice, closer now, said, "Samuel, Samuel."

Immediately, Samuel sat up and said, "Speak, God. Samuel, your servant, is listening."

God said, "I am going to do something in Israel so important that everyone's ears will tingle. I am going to punish Eli's

---

*This text also appears in Year B, Proper 4. The story can be used there as well.

family because he knows all the things his sons are doing wrong and doesn't stop them. "

Samuel could not go back to sleep. All he could think about were the words God said about Eli's family. He loved Eli, and he didn't want to tell him what God had said.

When morning came, Samuel opened the doors to the temple. Eli called to him, "Samuel, my son!"

"I'm here," said Samuel.

"What did God say to you?" Eli was excited to hear from Samuel. But Samuel didn't want to tell Eli.

"Tell me everything," said Eli. "Don't keep a single word from me."

And Samuel told Eli everything that God had said to him. He could see the sadness in Eli's eyes.

"God is the Lord," said Eli. "God will do as God pleases."

Samuel grew in the wisdom of God and was honest and truthful in God's ways as God's prophet.

Prayer: God who calls us, open our ears to hear your call to us through people around us. Make us ready to do what you ask. Amen.

A Reluctant Prophet of God
Jonah 3:1–5, 10*

Jonah," God said, "go to Nineveh and tell them to stop the evil that they do."

Jonah left sure enough, but he went in the opposite direction of Nineveh. Jonah hated the people of Nineveh, so he got on a ship headed to Tarshish. He thought he could run away from God. Silly Jonah!

God sent a storm into the path of the ship. The sailors thought they were going to die. When Jonah told them that his God was the creator of the sea and the dry land, they cried, "You did something to upset your God. It's your fault that we are going to die. What can we do?"

Jonah told them to throw him overboard, and they did. At that moment, the storm stopped, and the sailors all praised God.

But God sent an enormous fish that quickly swallowed Jonah. Jonah was in that fish's belly for three days. He prayed to God, and finally the fish spit him out.

However, God wasn't finished with Jonah. Again, God

*This story includes Jonah 1–3.

said, "Go to the great city of Nineveh. Give them the word of judgment that I have given you."

This time Jonah did go to Nineveh. When he got there, he walked through the city, yelling, "Nineveh will be destroyed in forty days!"

Much to Jonah's surprise, the people in Nineveh believed this message from God. Everyone, from the most important to the least important, from the largest to the smallest, even the cattle and all the animals, did not eat; and the people dressed in clothes that showed how sorry they were.

When God saw what the people of Nineveh were doing, God did not destroy the city and the people. Nineveh was saved.

Prayer: God of justice, we will try to listen to your word to us and do it as the people of Nineveh did. Amen.

A Teacher with Authority
Mark 1:21–28

After John the baptizer baptized Jesus, Jesus invited some men to travel with him. Now Jesus and his friends were in Capernaum. On the Sabbath day, the day of rest and worship for the Jews, Jesus went to the synagogue. He sat down and began to teach the people there.

While Jesus was teaching, a man came into the synagogue ranting and raving. In those days, he was said to have an evil spirit inside him, and he would not have been allowed inside the synagogue. But he was there and everything stopped.

The evil spirit screamed, "What are you doing, Jesus of Nazareth? I know you. You are the holy one of God."

"Quiet," yelled Jesus. "Evil spirit, come out of this man!" And it did!

The eyes of the people in the synagogue were wide, and their mouths hung open. "Who is this teacher with such authority in his words?" they asked. "Even evil spirits obey him."

News of this new teacher in the synagogue in Capernaum quickly spread from person to person and town to town, all over Galilee.

Prayer: Holy God, let us learn from the authority of Jesus so we too learn more about you. Amen.

Authority without Words
Mark 1:29–39

Peaople all over Capernaum were talking about Jesus' teaching. Jesus left the synagogue and went to the house of Simon and Andrew. James and John went with him.

As soon as they walked in the door, someone said to Jesus, "Simon's mother-in-law has a fever." Immediately Jesus went to her.

Unlike the way he healed the man with the evil spirit in the synagogue, Jesus didn't say a word to Simon's mother-in-law. He simply took her hand and helped her stand up.

As soon as the woman got up, the fever was gone, and she began to serve the guests: Jesus, James, and John.

When the sun began to set and the Sabbath day was over, people from all around brought sick friends and family members to Simon and Andrew's house. They crowded around the door. Jesus healed them all.

Early the next morning, before the sun came up, and while everyone was still asleep, Jesus left the house. He went to a quiet place where he could be alone to pray.

When Simon and the others got up, they couldn't find Jesus. When they finally found him, Simon said, "Jesus, everyone's looking for you!"

Simon may have sounded a little irritated, but Jesus just said, "Let's go to the other villages. I was sent to preach to them."

Jesus, Simon, Andrew, James, and John left that day. They traveled all over Galilee and Jesus preached in the synagogue in each town.

Prayer: Caring God, as Jesus prayed to you to learn what he was to do, so we pray to you to hear what you want us to do. In Jesus' name, we pray. Amen.

Along the Way
Mark 1:40–45

A man lived outside of town. He had a skin disease and was considered unclean. He was not allowed in the synagogue, and he couldn't have come to Simon and Andrew's house, where Jesus was, to be healed. His only hope was to find Jesus alone.

As the man came toward Jesus, Simon, Andrew, James, and John must have pulled back. They could see this man was sick and unclean.

When the man got to Jesus, he fell to his knees and said, "You can heal me, if you want to."

Jesus was so upset at the appearance of the man and his need to be healed that he took the man's hand. Surely, the men with Jesus gasped at the sight of him touching this unclean man.

Jesus said, "I want to heal you. Be clean."

With Jesus' words, the man's skin disease was gone. He was healed and no longer considered unclean. Now he could go to the synagogue, and people would not walk away from him.

*The Old Testament lection (2 Kings 5:1–14) can be found in *Feasting on the Word, Children's Sermons for Year C*, Proper 9.

Looking the man straight in the eye, Jesus said, "Don't tell anyone about this. Go to the priest and be made clean again according to the laws of Moses."

However, the man went away and told everyone he saw what had happened to him. The news of his healing traveled so fast that Jesus couldn't go into any town. When he did, he was surrounded by people. Instead Jesus stayed in the quiet places outside the towns. People from everywhere around came to him there.

It seemed impossible for Jesus to be alone.

Prayer: God of love and healing, we pray for all people who are sick and for the people who care for them. In Jesus' name, we pray. Amen.

A Dispute with Jewish Leaders
Mark 2:1–12

The house was packed. When people heard that Jesus was in town, they filled the house where he was staying. Not one more person could squeeze inside. In fact, so many people crowded around the door that you couldn't even see inside.

Jesus was teaching the people inside the house and anyone outside who could hear him.

Among the people who arrived who could not get in, there were four people who were carrying a man on a mat. This man was paralyzed; he could not move his legs. He couldn't stand up, and he couldn't walk. When they saw that they had no chance of getting their friend close to Jesus, they carried him up the outside stairs to the flat roof of the house.

They tore off some of the roof right above where Jesus was sitting. Don't you wonder what the people in the room thought as dust began to fall from the ceiling and then a man was lowered down from the roof?

But that's what happened. The four friends lowered the man who was paralyzed down to Jesus. When Jesus saw the faith of these friends, Jesus said to the paralyzed man, "Your sins are forgiven."

Right away some Jewish legal experts complained. "How can he forgive the man? Only God can forgive."

Jesus heard what they said and turned to them. "Why do you ask such questions? Is it easier to say to this man who cannot walk, 'Your sins are forgiven' or to say to him, 'Get up, pick up your mat, and walk'?"

Then Jesus said to the man, "Get up, pick up your mat, and go home."

Jesus helped the man get up. Then the man picked up his mat and walked out of the room. The people stood aside, amazed. Then they praised God and said, "We've never seen this kind of thing anywhere!"

I wonder what the Jewish legal experts were thinking.

Prayer: Loving and forgiving God, may we care for our friends as well as did the friends of the man who was paralyzed. In Jesus' name, we pray. Amen.

A New Disciple
Mark 2:13–22

After teaching and healing people, Jesus walked along the lake called the Sea of Galilee. No doubt he found the cool breeze off the lake refreshing and the waves on the lake calming after teaching and preaching to so many people. But he wasn't alone for long before a crowd of people found him. So he taught them as he walked along the shore.

When he came to a tax collector's booth, he stopped. Tax collectors were hated by the Jews because they worked for the Romans. They handled the money of the Roman government, which also made them unclean in the eyes of the Jews. They had few friends, mostly other tax collectors.

At this booth, Jesus said to the tax collector Levi, "Follow me."

Levi got up and went with Jesus.

That evening, Jesus and his disciples went to Levi's house for dinner. No matter where Jesus went now, people followed him. In the crowd outside Levi's house were some Jewish legal experts who were Pharisees. (Rules and laws were really important to them.) When they looked in the door and saw that Jesus was eating with tax collectors and other sinners, friends of Levi, they were angry. "Why is your master eating with tax collectors and sinners?" they asked Jesus' disciples.

The disciples didn't answer because Jesus did. He had heard the question. "Healthy people don't need doctors, and people who know God's ways don't need me to tell them about God. I have come to tell the people who *don't* know about God's ways and love."

Then Jesus turned back to the table in Levi's house to eat and talk with the people there.

Prayer: God of all people, may we and our church follow Jesus' example and enjoy the company of all people. In Jesus' name, we pray. Amen.

More Trouble with the Pharisees
Mark 2:23–3:6

On this Sabbath day, the day of rest, Jesus and his disciples were walking through a wheat field. Now you may wonder why they were walking through a wheat field. Although the Roman government had improved some major roads, there were few smaller roads, really what we might call trails. Sometimes the best way to get from one place to another was through a wheat field. I'm sure Jesus and the disciples were careful not to destroy the wheat plants, which were big enough to harvest.

As they walked, some of the disciples pulled the heads of wheat off the stems. And wouldn't you know that there were some Pharisees, letter-of-the-law guys, nearby, who saw this. Immediately, they cried, "These men are working on the Sabbath. They are harvesting this wheat!"

They hurried to Jesus. "Why are you letting your disciples work on the Sabbath? They are breaking the Sabbath law," they accused.

Perhaps Jesus smiled politely and said, "Don't you remember when David and his men were hungry? They took the bread of the presence that represented the twelve tribes of

Israel from the temple, which only the priests were to eat. David ate some and gave it to the men with him."

Those accusers may have looked a little embarrassed because Jesus continued. "The Sabbath was created for us, human beings; we were not created only to obey the Sabbath laws. This is why the one sent from God is Lord of the Sabbath."

Jesus and his followers kept going on the way to the synagogue in the next town. A man with a hand that he could not stretch out was there. The Pharisees were there too, watching Jesus very carefully to see if he would heal this man on the Sabbath.

Jesus stood in front of the people in the synagogue. He called to the man with the hand that wouldn't stretch, "Come right up here, in front where everyone can see you."

To everyone, but especially to the Pharisees, he said, "Is it right and lawful to do good or evil on the Sabbath?"

The room was silent. Jesus looked at the people with anger in his eyes. Could no one make way in their heart for good? To the man with the closed-up hand, he said, "Open your hand. Stretch the fingers."

Slowly, the man held up his hand and slowly he stretched his fingers until each one was straight. His hand was healed!

When they saw the man's hand was as good as new, the Pharisees began to plot to get rid of Jesus. Bad times ahead.

Prayer: Healing God, may we always be aware of the good we can do any day of the week. May we also remember that your way is a way of love. In Jesus' name, we pray. Amen.

❧ TRANSFIGURATION SUNDAY ❦
(LAST SUNDAY BEFORE LENT)

A Secret
*Mark 9:2–9**

Jesus called Peter (also known as Simon), James, and John over. "Come with me to the top of this mountain."

They started their climb. It was a very high mountain where they could be alone. Perhaps the three men thought they were going up the mountain to pray with Jesus. He seemed to like out-of-the-way places like this.

But when they got to the top of the mountain, Jesus' clothes began to shine like the brightest light, the hottest sun. The whiteness of his clothes sparkled like the sun on snow.

Then Elijah and Moses appeared and stood beside Jesus. The three talked together.

Not knowing what to do, Peter asked, "Shall I make three shelters, one for each of you? It's a good thing we are with you."

Nevertheless, Peter, James, and John were terrified at the sight of Jesus and the appearance of the two prophets.

Suddenly, a big cloud came over the top of the mountain. The men couldn't see one another. From the cloud, a voice

---

*The Old Testament lection (2 Kings 2:1–12) can be found in *Feasting on the Word, Children's Sermons for Year C*, Proper 8.

thundered, "This is my Son. I love him very much. Listen to him!"

In a flash, everyone was gone but Jesus, Peter, James, and John. Jesus' clothes were not sparkling and bright anymore.

The four men started down the mountain. On the way, Jesus said, "Don't tell anyone what you saw or heard on the top of the mountain. This is a secret until the one from God is raised from the dead."

What a secret!

Prayer: Holy God, you are powerful and awesome. We praise you. Amen.

Jesus' Rite of Passage
Mark 1:9–15

Every year on the Sunday after the Day of Epiphany, we celebrate the baptism of Jesus. This story for the first Sunday in Lent begins with Jesus' baptism from the Gospel of Mark. Mark tells it in just a few words.

"John was baptizing at the Jordan River. Jesus came from Nazareth to the river and John baptized him. After the baptism, Jesus saw the Holy Spirit, in the shape of a dove, come over him. A voice from above said, 'You are my son. I love you very much. You make me happy.'" That's it. But the next part of the story makes it an important story for the first Sunday in Lent, a season when we examine our lives as Jesus' disciples and our relationship to God.

Mark reports that right away, the Holy Spirit, which had just come over Jesus, led Jesus into the desert wilderness. Jesus was there for forty days. But this was no vacation camping trip. Jesus had taken no food with him and there was no place to get food. In the gospels of Matthew and Luke, we hear about the devil tempting Jesus three times and how Jesus answered the devil. In Mark, it just says that the devil, Satan, tempted Jesus.

Wild animals lived in the wilderness, and Jesus lived among them, according to Mark. Mark also says that angels took care of Jesus.

It's as if Mark is in a hurry to tell us about what Jesus taught and what Jesus did. But first, Mark wants us to know that Jesus was ready to do this. Jesus went through this rite of passage, a baptism and the time alone in the wilderness. Jesus was blessed by God at his baptism and watched over by God's angels in the wilderness. After this, Jesus began the work that God sent him to do. For this, we are thankful to God.

Prayer: God of all ages, we marvel at your love for us and your plan to hold Jesus and us in that love. Amen.

The Covenant with God Almighty
Genesis 17:1–7, 15–16

Abram and Sarai left their home and family when God called them to go to a new land. God promised that they would have many children. Years went by, and Abram and Sarai were ninety years old and still had no children. But they were faithful to God.

Now God came to Abram again. "I am El Shaddai, God Almighty. Walk with me. Trust me. I will keep my promise, my covenant with you. You will have many children, and they will have many children."

Recognizing that God Almighty had spoken, Abram fell to the ground in awe.

El Shaddai, God Almighty, said, "Because I have this promise for you, you will now be called Abraham, which means father of many nations. This promise will last forever. I will be your God and the God of all your children, generation after generation."

Abram, forever after this, would be known as Abraham, the father of many nations. But what about Sarai?

Then God Almighty said to Abraham, "You will no longer call your wife Sarai. From now on she will be Sarah. I will bless her, and she will have a son, even at her old age. From her son will come nations and leaders of nations."

Can you imagine what Abraham and Sarah talked about that night? A son, at their ages? But God Almighty did promise them, made a covenant with them. Just as they thought about that covenant and their relationship with God, so we think about our relationship with God during these days of Lent.

Prayer: El Shaddai, God Almighty, open our eyes to see and our ears to hear your promise for us. Then speak to our hearts that we may live faithfully as Abraham and Sarah did. Amen.

An Angry Jesus
John 2:13–22

People came to Jerusalem for Passover. Part of the celebration of that holiday was to bring animals to the temple as sacrifices. The animals had to be perfect, so many people bought their animals when they got to Jerusalem, where there were stalls with animals for sale. Other people sat at tables to exchange the Roman coins for temple coins, because the Roman coins couldn't be given to the temple.

We don't know what upset Jesus when he entered the courtyard of the temple, but he was pretty angry. He grabbed a piece of rope and whipped it around. Cows ran, sheep bleated, and doves flew from their cages. Tables fell over, and coins rolled all over the floor. It was chaos!

Jesus looked at the dove sellers. Pointing to them, Jesus said, "Get these cages and doves out of here! Don't make my Father's house a common store!"

Everyone in the temple looked on in astonishment. As Jesus' disciples watched all this fury and flurry, they remembered that the psalmist said, "Strong feelings for God's house have taken me."

Some Jewish leaders who had seen what Jesus did asked,

"Who gave you the power to do this? What miracle are you going to show us?"

"Tear down this temple and in three days I will build it again," said Jesus.

Almost laughing in his face, the Jewish leaders said, "It took forty-six years to build this temple. And you think you can rebuild it in three days?" They smiled at each other knowingly. Such a fool!

But Jesus was not talking about the temple building. No, Jesus was talking about himself. Until Jesus died and came back to life in three days, the disciples didn't understand what he was saying.

I wonder if others remembered Jesus' words.

Prayer: God of word and deed, we come to your house to worship you and to learn about you, especially through the stories of Jesus. Send your Spirit to us so we might listen carefully. In Jesus' name, we pray. Amen.

God's Gift
Ephesians 2:1–10

Today's story is from one of the letters in the New Testament. Letters were written to groups of Christians in places far from Jerusalem to correct and encourage them in their Christian faith and life. Imagine that you are part of a group of Christians in a place called Ephesus. Someone, maybe Paul, came to Ephesus a few years ago and told you about Jesus, the Christ. You became believers, but now it is hard to remember the teachings you heard. Imagine what it might be like to be part of a group of Christians, far away from other Christians and churches. How exciting it would be for a letter to arrive.

"Hello!" called voices as they entered the house. Today, the house church is to meet and everyone is gathering. They bring food to share—grapes, olives, bread, wine, goat cheese. The children are excited to see their friends and everyone is joyful. Today is special because a letter from one of the leaders who had begun their church has arrived.

Letters are not something that happen very often. A messenger has brought it on his way to another city. After everyone has something to eat, they gather together—men, women, and children.

Someone prays, praising and giving thanks to God. The leader of the house church, perhaps the only person who can read, stands up, unrolls the letter scroll, and reads:

"To the holy and faithful people in Christ Jesus in Ephesus.

"Grace and peace to you from God and from Jesus Christ.

"Before you learned about Jesus Christ, you acted like all the other people. You did whatever seemed good and whatever you wanted. But now you have a new life. This life was given to you by God through Jesus Christ. This new life wasn't a prize for something you did. No, it was a gift from God. You can't do anything to get this gift of new life from God. God gives it to you. Because you have this gift, you are able to do good things that show God's love in Jesus Christ."

Although there is more in the letter, the reader stops. What an amazing gift from God! People want to talk about the meaning of this gift. This is a gift they can show to others through the good things they do, just as Jesus taught and showed them.

Prayer: Gracious and giving God, thank you for the gift of your love as it is shown through Jesus Christ. We want to do the good things that show that we have received your gift of love. Amen.

A Comfort for All
Jeremiah 31:31–34

Jeremiah was a prophet of God during a time when God's people forgot about God.

The king of Babylon conquered God's people and took many of them to live in Babylon, far away from Jerusalem. This was a terrible time for God's people. God sent Jeremiah to give them hope. Listen to what Jeremiah told the people. Listen for words of comfort, words that would make them remember that they belong to God, words that would make them feel better.

"You, my people, forgot the commandments I gave you, written on the stone slabs when I brought you out of Egypt. We made a covenant that you would be my people and I would be your God. But you broke that promise, even though I was like a husband in that promise. We were that close.

"In this covenant, I will write the words on your hearts. We will be even closer than before. You will not have to teach them to anyone. My words will be in your heart. Everyone, from the youngest to the oldest, will be able to say, 'I know the LORD.'

"And I will forget all your sins and that you forgot about me. I will be your God, and you will be my people."

Jeremiah had many more words of comfort for the people, God's people of Israel and Judah. I wonder what the people thought of these words. I wonder what the people did to show that they remembered they were God's people.

Prayer: God of Comfort, when we forget that we are your people, remind us of these words that you gave Jeremiah for the people of Israel and Judah. Remind us that these words are for us too. Amen.

On a Colt
Mark 11:1–11

Today's story is in all four Gospels—Matthew, Mark, Luke, and John. It must be an important story, and it is one we tell every year on this Sunday, Palm Sunday.

Jesus and the disciples were walking toward Jerusalem, where they would celebrate the festival of Passover. They had been traveling for many days because people stopped Jesus to ask questions and beg him to heal people. When they finally reached Bethphage and Bethany, Jesus stopped at the Mount of Olives. When you stand on the Mount of Olives, you can look across to Jerusalem and see the big city walls. In Jesus' day, you could see the temple.

Perhaps the disciples thought that Jesus wanted a brief rest before walking down into the Kidron Valley and climbing up the other side to get to Jerusalem. It's a good idea because it is a bit of a hike on a hot day. Or perhaps they thought Jesus wanted to look at Jerusalem from a distance before they went into the city. Many people do pause to see this sight, even today.

But Jesus had another reason. Jesus called for two of the disciples, perhaps the two nearest to him. Jesus said to the two disciples, "Go into the village, just over there. You will see a young colt tied as soon as you enter. No one has ever ridden it. Bring it to me. If someone asks what you are doing, say, 'Its master needs it. He will send it back right away.'"

Perhaps a bit curious, the two disciples went off and did as Jesus told them. Sure enough, someone standing nearby asked, "What are you doing?"

They said exactly what Jesus told them to say and brought the colt to Jesus. They threw their outer clothes over the colt and Jesus sat on it. Off they went to Jerusalem. Down into the valley and up to the city walls of Jerusalem.

When they entered the city, people spread their clothes on the road and laid branches they cut from trees on the road. They shouted, "Hosanna! Blessings on the one who comes in God's name!"

When he reached the temple, Jesus got off the colt, went inside, and looked around at the beautiful temple. But it was already late in the day and the sun was going down, so Jesus and the disciples went back to Bethany to spend the night. And I suppose someone returned the colt to its owner.

Prayer: Holy God, on this Palm Sunday, we too welcome Jesus to Jerusalem. We want to follow his way of peace in today's world too. In Jesus' name, we pray. Amen.

Mary of Magdala, the First Evangelist
John 20:1–18

Everything was dark when Mary of Magdala, also known as Mary Magdalene, left the house. On this first day of the week, everything was quiet. We don't know why she headed to the tomb alone. Perhaps the pain of Jesus' death was so great that she wanted to be where he was laid. But when she got there, she saw that the great big stone, bigger than she was, had been pushed away from the opening of the burial cave.

Mary ran back to tell Simon Peter and the disciple that Jesus loved, "They have taken Jesus from the tomb. I don't know where his body is."

Simon Peter and the other disciple headed for the tomb. The closer they got the more they hurried, until they were running. The other disciple got there first. He looked inside and saw the linen cloth lying there, but he didn't go into the tomb.

When Simon Peter got there, he went inside. He saw the cloth that had been wrapped around Jesus' face at one end and the cloth wrapped around his body at the other end. Each cloth was folded neatly.

The other disciple came into the tomb. Both men saw and

believed what Mary Magdalene told them, but they didn't understand what had happened. They went back to the house where they were staying.

Meanwhile, Mary Magdalene had come back to the tomb. She stood outside it, crying. She bent down to look inside. To her surprise, she saw two angels dressed in white. One angel was sitting where Jesus' head would have been. The other was seated where his feet would have been. One of them said, "Woman, why are you crying?"

"They have taken Jesus away," she sobbed, "and I don't know where he is."

Something drew her attention, and she turned around and saw a man standing there. "Woman, why are you crying? Are you looking for someone?" he asked.

Mary thought this must be the gardener. Brushing her tears aside, she said, "If you have taken Jesus away, tell me and I will go to him."

"Mary," said the man.

As soon as the man said her name, Mary Magdalene knew who it was. "Teacher!" she cried.

"Don't touch me," said Jesus. "But go tell my brothers and sisters that I'm going to my Father, to their Father and God."

With that, Mary Magdalene hurried back to the house where the disciples were staying and announced, "I have seen the Lord! I have seen Jesus!" Then Mary Magdalene, the first one to see the risen Jesus, gave them his message.

Prayer: Glorious God, our joy is overwhelming as we hear the joyous message of Mary Magdalene: "I have seen Jesus!" We praise you on this Easter Day for your everlasting love and promise. Amen and amen.

Of One Heart and Soul
Acts 4:32–35

So what did those first followers of Jesus do after the risen Jesus appeared? First, they waited in Jerusalem for the gift of the Holy Spirit, as Jesus told them to do. When the Holy Spirit came to them on the day of Pentecost, the disciples began to tell others the good news of God's love through Jesus the Christ. In a very short time, the number of believers in Jesus the Christ had grown to five thousand. Imagine!

Surely not all of them stayed in Jerusalem, but many did. There were Jews and Gentiles, people who were not Jewish. They spoke Greek, Aramaic, and maybe other languages. They were young and old, children and adults. They were different in many ways. But the Jews still went to the temple to pray, and probably some of the Gentiles were used to doing that too. They were together under the leadership of the disciples, also called the apostles.

And they had one important thing in common. Everyone had been baptized with the Holy Spirit, and this was very important. This made it possible for them to be of "one heart and soul" as it is recorded in the book of the Acts of the Apostles, usually called Acts for short.

These new believers brought what they had and shared it with people who had nothing or very little. They did this happily because they were of "one heart and soul."

When it was needed, people who owned land or a house sold it and brought the money to the apostles so it could be used for the good of everyone. They did it happily because they were of "one heart and soul."

And all the time, the apostles continued to witness, to tell others about the powerful message of God's love through Jesus the Christ. This love was at work through the apostles and all the new believers, all five thousand of them.

Prayer: Loving God, we know most of us don't live exactly like these early believers. But we pray that we can live together with one heart and soul and that we can be as generous as they were in order that every person has what she or he needs. In Jesus' name, we pray. Amen.

More Witnesses to the Risen Jesus
Luke 24:36b–48

On Easter Sunday, the story was about Mary of Magdala, known as Mary Magdalene, who was the first person in the Gospel of John to see Jesus after he rose from death. Today's story is about other disciples seeing Jesus later that same day.

Cleopas and another disciple, perhaps his wife, entered the house where the disciples were staying, eager to tell them about seeing Jesus on their way to Emmaus. But they quickly discovered that everyone was talking about Simon Peter seeing him too.

As the people talked excitedly, Jesus suddenly stood in front of them. "Peace be with you," he said to them. Despite all their stories about seeing Jesus, they were frightened and wondered if they were seeing a ghost.

Seeing their faces, Jesus asked, "Why are you surprised? Why are you uncertain? Look at the scars on my hands and my feet. It's me! Touch me. You can't touch a ghost."

Jesus showed them his hands and feet. Because they still seemed a little uncertain, Jesus said, "Get me something to eat."

Someone handed Jesus baked fish, and he ate it, just like any person would. This was not a ghost!

"Remember what I said to you?" asked Jesus, "I said that everything written in the prophets, the books of Moses, and in the Psalms would come true."

Then they began to remember and their hearts were open to what he was telling them now.

"It is written that the Messiah, the Christ, must die and will rise again on the third day. After that a message of change of heart and forgiveness of sins must be preached. You are the ones to do this all over, beginning in Jerusalem. You are witnesses. You have seen and heard all these things. But stay in Jerusalem until you receive the gift of the Holy Spirit, which will come from God."

Now not only Mary of Magdala had seen the risen Jesus, but the disciples had too. Now they had a job, a mission to do for Jesus and God.

Prayer: Holy One, we are thankful that all those who were given the mission to spread your good news did so. We will continue that mission today. In Jesus' name, we pray. Amen.

Leaping and Praising God
Acts 4:5–12*

As you remember, Jesus and the disciples were all Jews. As faithful Jews, the Twelve continued to worship at the temple each day after Jesus went to heaven, leaving them to carry out his mission.

One day Peter and John were on their way to the temple for the three o'clock prayers. They did this every day. At the same time a man who couldn't walk was being carried to the temple. He sat at the Beautiful Gate (that was the name of the gate) of the temple every day at this time to ask people for money as they were going to pray. On this day, he was settled by the Beautiful Gate before Peter and John arrived at the temple. He called to them, "Money, please! Money for a man who can't walk!"

The two disciples looked at the man for a long moment. You might say they stared at him, like they had never seen him before.

"Look here," called Peter. "Look at us!"

The man who couldn't walk looked at Peter and John. He expected them to give him some money.

---

*This story is based on Acts 3:1–10, which tells of the healing that brought Peter and John before the Jewish leaders, as recounted in Acts 4:5–12.

"We have no money," said Peter. "But I will give you what I have. In the name of Jesus, get up and walk!"

Then Peter took the man by the hand and helped him stand up. Immediately, his ankles and legs became strong, like he had been walking for days. He began to walk around. When he realized that he really could walk, he began to hop and leap. All the time he praised God.

All this to-do caught the attention of other people coming to the temple to pray at three o'clock. They recognized the man as the one who couldn't walk and who sat by the Beautiful Gate every day asking for money. The people were surprised, really surprised to see this man hopping and jumping and leaping. What could have happened to this man?

Prayer: God of surprises, open our eyes to see your surprises around us each day, in the morning, in the afternoon, at three o'clock, and in the evening. In Jesus' name, we pray. Amen.

Sent to Witness
Acts 8:26–40

"Be my witnesses. Tell about me in all Judea and Samaria and to the end of the earth." These were Jesus' last words to the disciples. When they did this in Jerusalem, as when Peter healed the man at the temple gate who could not walk, they got into trouble with the Jewish leaders and with the Roman government. Many people left Jerusalem for other places and took the story of Jesus with them.

When so many people became believers in Jesus, the apostles couldn't do all the work. So they appointed seven men to help them. One of these men was Philip, who became known as Philip the evangelizer, which means that he told people the good news of Jesus the Christ. Today's story is about Philip.

It begins when Philip is preaching in a city in Samaria. He was doing just fine there when an angel of God said to him, "Go to the road that goes from Jerusalem." Now this was a road through the desert wilderness, a dangerous road, especially if you were traveling by yourself. The angel gave more instructions: "Leave at noon." Oh boy, the hottest time of the day! But Philip did what the angel said. At noon, he started down the road that goes from Jerusalem to Gaza. And it was hot!

On this same road from Jerusalem to Gaza was a man

from Ethiopia. He had come to Jerusalem to worship God, but now he was on his way home. He was the treasurer of all the money that belonged to the queen of Ethiopia. This man had an important job, which explains why he was riding in a chariot, not walking like many travelers did. As he sat in his chariot, riding along, the man was reading a scroll of the book of Isaiah.

Now Philip could see this man in the chariot. The Holy Spirit said to Philip, "Go to the chariot and keep up with it."

Philip ran up alongside the chariot. He listened and recognized that the man was reading from Isaiah.

"Do you understand what you are reading?" Philip asked. The chariot stopped.

"It's confusing," said the man. "How can I figure this out without someone to help me? If you can help me, get up into my chariot."

Philip got into the chariot. They started off as Philip explained to the man about Isaiah. Then he told the man about Jesus the Christ.

Before long, they were passing by some water.

"Look at that water," said the man. "Is there any reason why I can't be baptized here?"

They stopped. Philip and the man from Ethiopia got out of the chariot and walked to the water. Philip baptized the man. Then the Holy Spirit took Philip to Azotus where he continued to preach about Jesus the Christ. Don't you think the Ethiopian man went home to tell everyone what had happened and the good news of Jesus the Christ? He became the first witness to the good news of Jesus in Ethiopia.

Prayer: God of all people, just as many people have been your witnesses through the years, guide us to be your witnesses today. In Jesus' name, we pray. Amen.

❧ SIXTH SUNDAY OF EASTER ❧

Baptisms in Caesarea
Acts 10:44–48

God spoke to Cornelius, a Roman soldier, and told him to send people to bring Peter to Caesarea. So Cornelius sent people to get Peter from a town called Joppa, where Peter was staying with Simon the tanner.

Peter took some Jewish believers like himself with him to be witnesses.

When they got to the house of Cornelius, the family and neighbors of Cornelius were waiting for Peter. They were excited to hear what Peter had to tell them.

Now this may sound like an ordinary story of how the good news of Jesus the Christ was spread from city to city. Yes, it is. But it is also a special story. Remember that Peter and the disciples and the Jewish believers still followed the laws of Moses. One law was not to have anything to do with people who were not Jewish, and especially with the Roman soldiers who had invaded their land. But Cornelius wasn't like most of the Roman soldiers. Cornelius believed in the Lord God. He wasn't Jewish, but he worshiped God.

When Peter entered the house of Cornelius, Cornelius bowed down to Peter. "No, no," said Peter. "I'm just a man like you. Don't bow down to me."

When Peter saw all the people who had gathered to greet him, he was surprised. "You know," he said, "we Jews don't come to your houses, you who aren't Jewish. But God has shown me that everything created by God is good. So I have come to Caesarea, and here I am in this house. But tell me why you sent for me."

Cornelius said, "Four days ago at three o'clock in the afternoon I was praying. God told me to send for you at the house of Simon in Joppa. It was because God had seen the good things I have done for people here. So I did, and here you are. We are ready to hear what you have to tell us."

Peter looked at the people, eagerly waiting to hear his words. He told them all about Jesus the Christ and how Jesus had told the disciples to witness to people everywhere. Meanwhile the Jewish believers who had come with Peter looked around in astonishment at what was happening.

"And everyone who believes in Jesus can be forgiven by God," Peter ended.

At that moment the Holy Spirit came over Cornelius and his family and neighbors. The Jewish believers from Joppa were amazed at this sight and the sound of them praising God.

"These people have been given the Holy Spirit. They can be baptized," said Peter.

The people were all baptized and Peter stayed with them for several days. What a time they must have had!

Prayer: God of all creation, open our hearts to your Holy Spirit as the people in Caesarea did. In Jesus' name, we pray. Amen.

A Rooted Tree
Psalm 1*

If you open your Bible to the middle, you probably open it to the book of Psalms. You know right away that this book is different from most others in the Bible. It looks like poetry. And it is. A psalm is a song to God. Songs are poems with music. But we don't have the music that goes with the psalms in the Bible. However, we do sing psalms when we come here to worship God. Musicians have written music so that we can sing them together.

But even when we aren't singing psalms, we can read them and learn about God from them. The very first psalm tells us right away what God wants us to do and what will make us truly happy.

Listen for what that is:

> "If you want to be truly happy,
>> don't listen to the words of people who
>>> do wrong
>> and don't hang out with a bad gang.

*Psalm 1 is also the psalm for Year A, Proper 25; Year B, Easter 7 and Proper 20; and Year C, Epiphany 6 and Proper 18.

"No, do this:
    follow the way of God found in God's
        commandments.
    Learn them so you can say them day and night.
"The person who does this is like a tree planted by
        a flowing stream of water.
"The person who does this is truly happy in all that
        she or he does.
"But look at the people who don't know and follow
        God's way:
    they have no idea where they are going,
    no one believes what they say.
"God knows exactly what the truly
        happy person does
    and is glad.
"But God is not pleased with the ways of those
        who ignore God's way."

Prayer: God of love, we want to be truly happy and to follow in your ways. Teach us your ways and give us the courage to follow them. Amen.

The Big Bang of the Church
Acts 2:1–21

Passover was over long ago. The disciples chosen by Jesus were still waiting in Jerusalem. Jesus promised that they would receive the Holy Spirit. Then they could take the good news of God's love and the story of Jesus the Christ to all parts of the world. They waited and waited. Now it was almost time to celebrate the festival of Pentecost. Jews from all over came to Jerusalem for this festival. How much longer were the disciples going to have to wait?

The wait was almost over. On Pentecost Day the Twelve and other disciples were all together in one room in Jerusalem. Perhaps they were eating together, or maybe they were remembering times when Jesus taught them or healed someone. Whatever they were doing, they stopped when a strong, howling wind interrupted them. At the same time, little flames danced over each person's head. What a sight!

At that very minute, they were all filled with the Holy Spirit, just as Jesus promised them. Each of them began to tell the good news of Jesus the Christ. But they were speaking in languages they couldn't speak before. Some spoke the language of the Medes; some, the Parthians; others, Mesopotamians; and still others, even more different languages.

Of course, all these voices jumbled together attracted the attention of people on the street outside the house. They looked in the door and peeked in the windows. "What is going on?" they asked one another.

Then someone said, "That person is speaking my language, but he isn't from my country." And others began to say the same thing. The people outside looked at one another with confusion in their eyes. One person laughed and said, "They must be drinking new wine."

Peter saw the crowd that had gathered outside the house. He heard the comment about new wine. "Friends," he said, "it's only nine o'clock in the morning. We are not drunk on new wine. We have received the Holy Spirit. This is what God told the prophet Joel. This is a wonderful day!"

When everyone was listening, Peter told the people about Jesus the Christ. That day about three thousand people believed and were baptized. What a way for the church of Jesus Christ to begin!

Prayer: God of wind and fire, on this Pentecost Day when we celebrate the beginning of the church, we thank you for the gift of the Holy Spirit to those early believers and believers through all the years. Amen.

A Fantastical Story
Isaiah 6:1–8

Do you ever close your eyes and imagine what a story looks like when someone is reading or telling it? This story is a good one to imagine. It is a fantastical story!

It all happened in the year that King Uzziah of Judah died. God needed a prophet, someone new. For some reason, Isaiah was in the temple in Jerusalem at just the right time.

He saw God sitting on a throne high up near the ceiling. God's robe spread out over the whole floor and filled the temple. The edges of it touched the walls.

Around God were six-winged creatures called seraphim. With two wings, they covered their faces. With two more wings, they covered their feet. And with two more wings, they flew around God.

They shouted to one another, like a chant:

"Holy, holy, holy is the God of the heavenly forces!
"The earth, all of it, is filled with God's glory!"

The sound of their voices was loud, so loud that the frames of the doors shook! Smoke filled the room.

Isaiah was terrified. "I'm no good. I have said words I should not have said. I live with people who do wrong things. How is it that I have seen God?"

Then one of the six-winged creatures flew to Isaiah. It was carrying a hot coal from the altar. It touched Isaiah's lips with the hot coal, but his lips were not hurt. The creature said to Isaiah, "See, I touched your lips with this hot coal. The words you said are gone. You are clean!"

Isaiah jumped when God spoke: "Whom shall I send? Who will go for us?"

"I'm right here," said Isaiah. "Send me."

And that was the beginning of a long adventure for Isaiah, a prophet of God.

Prayer: God of majesty, you are so awesome! We praise you every day, and we want to be those who will go for you. Amen.

🎝 PROPER 3 / EPIPHANY 8 🎝
(Sunday between May 24 and May 28 inclusive, if after Trinity Sunday)

A Determined Missionary
*2 Corinthians 3:1–6**

Paul is known as a great missionary who traveled from country to country to tell people about Jesus the Christ. One of the places he went was Corinth. In Corinth, he met a couple, Aquila and his wife, Priscilla. They had been run out of Rome because all Jews were ordered to leave. They were tentmakers as Paul was, so Paul often worked with them while he was in Corinth. He stayed with them too.

But the most important work Paul did was to preach in the synagogue, telling the story of Jesus the Christ to Jews and Greeks. After his friends Silas and Timothy came to Corinth, Paul spent all his time telling about Jesus the Christ.

Sometimes people made fun of Paul. Then he just ignored them and went to someone else. The Jews in the synagogue didn't listen to him, so Paul taught next door at the home of Titius Justus. This did not make the leaders of the synagogue happy at all. They tried to have Paul arrested by the Roman government. During all this uproar, God told Paul not to give up. And because Paul didn't give up, many people

---

*This story tells about Paul's time in Corinth from Acts 18, providing background for the epistle reading. The story for the Gospel lesson (Mark 2:13–22) can be found at the Eighth Sunday after the Epiphany.

in Corinth, even some leaders of the synagogue, listened to Paul and became believers in Jesus the Christ.

Paul stayed in Corinth for eighteen months. After he left, he wrote letters to the church he had begun in Corinth. This is how he continued to teach them after he left. There are two letters to the church in Corinth in the New Testament of our Bible. We call them First and Second Corinthians.

Prayer: Gracious God, you told Paul not to give up. We want to be faithful to you, as he was. Amen.

(Sunday between May 29 and June 4 inclusive,
if after Trinity Sunday)

SEMICONTINUOUS

Keep the Sabbath
*Deuteronomy 5:12–15**

You may have heard the story of the Ten Commandments. The Hebrews lived as slaves in Egypt so long that
they forgot how to live together in God's ways. So God gave
Moses the Ten Commandments written on stone slabs. The
people could see them and remember them. The Old Testament lesson today is about one of the Ten Commandments.
So it isn't really a story.

Usually we read the Ten Commandments from the book
of Exodus, which tells about the long journey (forty years!)
from slavery in Egypt to freedom in Canaan. But the Ten
Commandments are also in the book of Deuteronomy, which
means "second law." In the book of Deuteronomy, Moses
summarizes all the ways the people are to live in God's ways.

Today we are going to think about just one commandment: Keep the Sabbath day for it is a holy day. On it do
exactly what God commanded.

The Sabbath day was the seventh day of the week, the day
we call Saturday. The Sabbath day for Christians, people like

---

*The Old Testament lesson for the semicontinuous stream [1 Samuel 3:1–10, (11– 20)] is on
the Second Sunday after the Epiphany. The Gospel lesson for this day (Mark 2:23–3:6) is
on the Ninth Sunday after the Epiphany (along with this text from Deuteronomy).

us, is Sunday. So I am going to say Sunday instead of Sabbath, but you know that if you read this in your Bible, it will say Sabbath.

Keep Sunday a holy day. Remember when God's people were slaves in Egypt. The Pharaoh told the slave masters to make them work every day. They had not one day off. And the work kept getting harder and harder. "Make more bricks," the slave masters shouted. "Gather your own straw to make them and make twice as many today." It was a terrible time for the Hebrews, God's people.

God saw what was happening. God had a plan to free the people from Pharaoh and the slave masters. But God did not want the people to forget how horrible life was as slaves in Egypt. So the commandment to keep the Sabbath, to keep Sunday, is all about resting on that day, something they couldn't do in Egypt. And everyone, absolutely everyone, including the animals, was to rest. The field workers, the oxen, the bakers, the cooks, everyone was to rest. No work!

But that wasn't all. Sunday, the Sabbath, is a holy day. God told the people that they were to rest and to worship God. This day of rest is a gift from God, so we are to give thanks to God and worship God on this day. You are doing that this morning, right now. You are following the commandment: keep the Sabbath holy.

So this day, Sunday, is a day of rest and of remembering God. It is a holy day when we worship God. It is a day when we rest instead of work. Thanks be to God.

Prayer: God of the Sabbath, we praise you for this holy day. We honor you for this gift of rest. We adore you for this break in our week. Amen.

(Sunday between June 5 and June 11 inclusive,
if after Trinity Sunday)

SEMICONTINUOUS

A Demand for a King They Could See
1 Samuel 8:4–11 (12–15), 16–20 (11:14–15)

Samuel was the judge over Israel. He was chosen by God because the sons of Eli, the judge before Samuel, cheated and didn't follow God's ways. Now the same thing was happening to Samuel. He also had two sons. He appointed them as judges, and they cheated and did all kinds of things that weren't according to God's ways.

The people had had enough. The elders, the leaders of Israel, came to Samuel. "Samuel, you are getting old. Your sons are terrible, unfair, dishonest judges. We do not want them. They have turned out just like Eli's sons. We don't see anyone who can take your place. We want a king that we can see, like all the other nations have. Give us a king to judge us."

Samuel did not think this was a good idea. He prayed, "God, they are asking for a king. What should I do?"

God's answer was that Samuel should give the people a king, but he should tell them what a king could do to them and their children.

Samuel called the elders of Israel together. "God told me to give you a king. But you must know that a king will take your sons and make them fight for him. A king will take your daughters to work in the palace. A king can take your best

72

fields and give them to his favorite people. Every year a king will take part of your harvest of grain and part of your herds and flocks. The king has the power to make you slaves. Then you will cry to God for help and mercy."

The people paid no attention to what Samuel said. They shouted, "We want a king! We want a king! We want a king like other nations have. We want a king who will be our judge. We want a king who will lead us in battle!"

Samuel returned to God and told God what the people said. "Give them a king," said God.

After a while, Saul was crowned the king of Israel and everyone celebrated. I wonder how that worked out.

Prayer: God of majesty, you rule over us and judge us with mercy. We praise you. Amen.

(Sunday between June 5 and June 11 inclusive,
if after Trinity Sunday)

GOSPEL

A Big Family
Mark 3:20–35

The sun was setting, and Jesus had spent a long day teaching and healing. He wanted nothing more than to sit down with the twelve disciples and relax over a meal.

But when he went into a house, a crowd quickly gathered there. It was impossible for him and the Twelve to eat anything.

Meanwhile, Jesus' family had heard about the things Jesus was doing and the crowds that were following him. From what they were told, they wondered if he might be out of his mind. So they decided to go to him; perhaps he would come home to Nazareth with them.

Back at the house where Jesus was, some Jewish religious leaders had come down from Jerusalem. They thought Jesus was working with Satan, the devil, evil.

Jesus, as tired and hungry as he was, had to explain to them. "If Satan were in me, how could I throw Satan out of others? A house divided into pieces will fall down."

Jesus continued to explain that he was from God, but the religious leaders kept saying, "He has an evil spirit."

As this was going on, Jesus' mother and brothers showed

up. They were unable to get inside the house where Jesus was, so they sent a message to him that they were outside.

When Jesus got the message, he looked at the people around him. "Who are my mother and brothers? You are my mother and brothers. Anyone who does God's will is my mother, my brother, my sister."

At first it sounds like Jesus is being rude to his mother and brothers. But I wonder if he is saying that they and everyone else who does God's will is like a mother, a brother, or a sister to him. What do you think?

Prayer: God of all people, help us to live so we are brothers or sisters to Jesus and children of yours. In Jesus' name, we pray. Amen.

❧ PROPER 6 ☙
(Sunday between June 12 and June 18 inclusive,
if after Trinity Sunday)

SEMICONTINUOUS

A New King
1 Samuel 15:34–16:13

The new king Saul was fine for a while, but then things didn't go so well. God decided to take his spirit from Saul and get a new king. Samuel had high hopes for King Saul. He was sad that Saul had turned away from God. He sat and moped about the way things were.

"Samuel," God said. "Snap out of it! Are you going to sit around and mope about Saul forever? It's time to replace him with a king who will follow my ways. Fill your horn with oil and get moving. Go to Bethlehem where Jesse lives. He has many sons. One of them will be the new king."

"But God," said Samuel, "what if Saul finds out? He will kill me!"

"Take a young cow with you and say you are going to make a sacrifice to me. Invite Jesse and his sons to go with you. I will give you a signal so that you will know which son to anoint."

Samuel filled his animal horn with oil to anoint the new king. He took a young cow and left for Bethlehem. When he got there, the village rulers, or elders, met him. He could tell that they were worried about his presence. But Samuel said, "I've come to make a sacrifice. Get ready and come with me."

Then Samuel looked around to be sure that Jesse and his sons were coming too.

At the place for the sacrifice, Samuel looked at the oldest son Eliab. *What a strong young man! He would be a good king,* thought Samuel.

But God said to Samuel alone, "No, I don't look at the outside of people. I look inside at the heart."

Samuel turned to the second son of Jesse, Abinadab. But God said, "No, I don't look at the outside of people. I look inside at the heart."

Then came Shammah, but again God said, "No, I don't look at the outside of people. I look inside at the heart."

Samuel had met seven of Jesse's sons, and each time God said, "No, I don't look at the outside of people. I look inside at the heart."

"Jesse," said Samuel, "do you have any more sons?"

"Well, yes," said Jesse. "There is one more. My youngest son is in the field near here watching the sheep."

"Send for him immediately. We will wait," said Samuel.

When David came, Samuel could see that he was a handsome young man. Perhaps Samuel worried that he was not the one. But God said, "Yes, anoint David. But remember that I look inside at the heart."

Samuel asked David to kneel and Samuel poured the oil over David's head. At that very moment, the spirit of God came to David and stayed with him. And Samuel went back home. Surely he wondered what would happen to this new king, chosen by God.

Prayer: God of surprising choices, we pray that when you look inside our hearts, you see how much we praise you and want to live in your ways. Amen.

*(Sunday between June 12 and June 18 inclusive,
if after Trinity Sunday)*

GOSPEL

God's Kingdom
Mark 4:26–34

For Jesus, it was another busy day of teaching crowds of people. Now Jesus was alone with the twelve disciples and a few others. He was explaining the stories, the parables he had told the crowd earlier in the day. The people listening had asked why he taught with parables and what did they mean.

Patiently, Jesus explained that he told parables so those people who really wanted to understand what God's kingdom, or world, was like would know.

Then he told two more short parables:

"God's world is like this: You plant seed in the ground. You go to sleep and wake up in the morning. You do this over and over, forgetting about the seed you planted. In the ground that seed sprouts and sends roots into the earth. But you can't see it yet. Then you see a little plant coming up out of the ground. It grows bigger and bigger until you have a big plant that has blossoms and vegetables. When the vegetables are the right size, you pick them and eat them.

"Or God's world is like this: Look at the mustard seed. It is such a teeny, tiny seed that you can barely see it. You plant it in the ground and one day it comes up. Day after day, it grows. Before you know it, you have a plant that is big enough for birds to find shade in it. All of that plant from that teeny, tiny seed."

Now Jesus told many more parables like these two. People who were ready to hear them learned about God's world from them. Sometimes the disciples didn't understand, and Jesus explained the parables to the disciples when they were alone.

Prayer: Creating God, open our ears to hear the stories Jesus told so long ago in order that we will know more about your world as you want it to be. In Jesus' name, we pray. Amen.

*(Sunday between June 19 and June 25 inclusive,
if after Trinity Sunday)*

SEMICONTINUOUS

A Challenge Met

1 Samuel 17:(1a, 4–11, 19–23), 32–49

"David," said Jesse, his father, "go to the valley where your brothers are fighting for King Saul against the Philistines. Take this bread and cheese to them. Come back and tell me how they are doing."

The next morning, David got up early and started off to where the battle was taking place. He got there just as the soldiers were lining up to fight. David left the bags of food to go see where his brothers were. When he found them, he saw the giant Goliath and heard Goliath challenge Israel's army. This happened every day, and it had gone on for forty days. David was a young man, perhaps a teenager; Goliath was nearly nine feet tall.

David asked some soldiers about this and why no one would battle with Goliath. Saul heard about David and sent for him.

"I will fight Goliath," said David.

"You can't do that," said Saul. "You are a boy with no experience in battle. Goliath has been fighting since he was your age."

"I have battled lions and bears who wanted to kill the sheep," said David. "This Philistine giant will just be like killing a lion or a bear because he insults the army of the living God."

"Then do it," said Saul. He gave David his armor and shield, but they were much too big for David.

"I can't move in this," said David. "I will use what I always use, my slingshot and stones."

David picked five smooth stones from the river bed. Off to meet Goliath!

When Goliath saw David, he laughed. "What? You send a boy to fight me?"

"You stand there with spear and shield, but I come with God on my side," called David.

With that, David put a stone in his slingshot. He slung it, and it hit Goliath on his forehead where there was no protection. The giant Goliath fell over dead.

When the Philistine army saw what had happened, they ran away.

Prayer: Powerful God, you were with David, and he defeated the giant. You had great plans for David, just as you have great plans for each of us. Amen.

(Sunday between June 19 and June 25 inclusive,
if after Trinity Sunday)

GOSPEL

A Storm at Sea
Mark 4:35–41

A little breeze was coming off the Sea of Galilee as Jesus
and the twelve disciples were winding up a busy day.
Jesus had taught a crowd of people and then talked with the
disciples and a few other people.

It wasn't dark yet. Jesus said, "Let's go to the other side of
the sea."

So Jesus and the Twelve piled into a boat and started
across to the other side. Other boats followed them. Jesus,
tired from the day and relaxed by the cool breeze on the
water, fell asleep.

Perhaps some of the disciples were drowsy too. Perhaps
they were thinking about the parables Jesus had told the
crowds or the one about the mustard seed that Jesus told
them.

Suddenly, a strong wind started blowing. This happened
often on the Sea of Galilee, but this wind felt stronger than
usual. Even the fishermen on board began to worry. However, Jesus just kept sleeping.

Waves were big, and water washed into the boat. The pas-
sengers were thrown from side to side. Were they going to
drown?

Jesus was still asleep in the back of the boat, on a pillow!

Some of the disciples shook Jesus to wake him. "How can you sleep through all this?" they asked. "Don't you care that we could drown?"

Jesus shook the sleep from his head. Calmly, he said, "Silence, be still!"

With those words, the wind stopped. There was barely enough breeze to keep the boat moving toward the shore.

Jesus looked at the men he had chosen to be his disciples. "Why were you so afraid? Are you still without faith?"

The disciples were speechless. Awesome! "He can even control the wind," they said. "Who is this man?"

How would you answer their question?

Prayer: God of the wind, through these stories in the Gospel of Mark, open our hearts and minds to who Jesus is. Amen.

A Story within a Story
Mark 5:21–43

"Let's go back to the other side of the sea to Capernaum," Jesus said to the disciples. No wind storm on this trip. When they got there, a large crowd quickly surrounded Jesus as he got out of the boat. How did they know he was coming?

Jairus, a leader in the synagogue, stepped out of the crowd and came toward Jesus. When he reached Jesus, Jairus fell to his knees. "Please, come to my house. My twelve-year-old daughter is dying," he pleaded. "Only you can save her."

Jesus walked with Jairus. The people followed and crowded in around Jesus, making it difficult for him to walk.

At the edge of the crowd was a woman who had been sick for twelve years. She mumbled to herself, "If I can only touch his robe, I will be healed." She had already spent all of her money on doctors, and they had done no good. Jesus was her last hope. She pushed and wiggled her way through the people until she could just reach out her hand and touch Jesus' robe. When she did, she knew immediately that she was healed. "I knew it," she said to herself.

At that same moment, Jesus stopped. "Who touched me?" he asked. A disciple said, "All kinds of people are touching you in this crowd that is so close to you. What do you mean?"

Jesus looked at the crowd, searching the face of each person. The woman was shaking because she was afraid that Jesus was angry. She fell down before Jesus and said, "I have been sick for twelve years. I paid all my money to doctors. Still they didn't heal me, but I knew that you could."

Jesus smiled kindly at her and said, "Daughter, your faith has made you well. Go in peace."

The woman went home, and Jesus continued on to the house of Jairus. They hadn't gone very far when some of Jairus's servants ran to him. "She has died," they said. "There is no reason for Jesus to come."

Jesus heard them. "Nonsense, just keep trusting," he said. Then Jesus called Peter, James, and John to go with him.

When they got to the house, people were crying and shouting. "Why all this noise?" asked Jesus. "The girl is just asleep."

The people laughed at him. He sent them all out, and not very politely. "Out, out!"

Then, Jesus told the girl's parents and the three disciples to come with him to where the girl was. Jesus took her hand. "Girl, get up."

Right away the girl sat up, and Jesus helped her stand. The girl's parents and the disciples couldn't believe their eyes!

"Don't tell anyone what you saw," ordered Jesus. "Now get this girl some food."

I wonder if the girl's parents, who must have been so excited, could keep from telling what happened to their daughter.

Prayer: God of healing, thank you for the many ways of healing we have today. Thank you for all the people who try to find new ways of healing too. Amen.

(Sunday between July 3 and July 9 inclusive)

SEMICONTINUOUS

King of Judah and Israel
2 Samuel 5:1–5, 9–10

When Samuel anointed that young shepherd David as king of Israel, David didn't become king right away. But when King Saul died, and his sons died too, David became king of Judah, some of God's people. There was another king of Israel, the rest of God's people. Seven years went by and that king died.

The leaders, the elders, of Israel had surely heard about King David, and they liked what they heard. A group of elders came to David in Hebron, where he lived.

"Look, we are part of God's people too. We are all relatives, family. When King Saul was alive, you led us in battle, and we won. And didn't God tell you that you would be the shepherd of Israel, the leader of Israel? We want you to be our king too."

David listened to the elders. They were right. God had told him that he would be the shepherd of Israel, of all God's people. Now was the moment. So the elders from Israel and David made a covenant in the presence of God. David was thirty years old when he became king of all Israel (Judah and Israel together).

But Hebron, where he lived, was too far south to be the king's home for all Israel. So King David moved to Jerusalem, which became known as David's City. He ruled in Jerusalem for more than thirty years. During that time God was with David, and he became more and more powerful. The shepherd boy who became king of Judah was the most famous king of all Israel.

Prayer: Almighty God, you were with David as he was king over your people. Be with the leaders of all countries in your world today. Amen.

Disciples on the Move
Mark 6:1–13

Jesus and the twelve disciples left Capernaum on the shore of the Sea of Galilee and went to Nazareth where Jesus had grown up. On the Sabbath day they went to the synagogue with everyone else. But things didn't go well. The people just couldn't think of Jesus as anything other than the boy they had known when he lived there. They didn't believe in him, so he and the disciples left.

Jesus taught in some small towns around the area, and then he had a plan. He sat down with the twelve disciples and told them what he wanted them to do.

"Choose a partner. I have a plan for you to go out in my name and heal the people," said Jesus.

Can you imagine the surprise on the faces of the disciples? Did they know enough? Did they have the ability to heal?

"I will give you the power to heal. You have heard me teach."

The disciples felt a little better. But still.

"Don't take anything with you but a walking stick. Wear sandals, but don't put on an extra shirt. No food, no extra clothing, and no money."

Now the disciples didn't feel quite so sure.

"When you are invited into a house, stay there until you leave that town. But if the town isn't friendly to you, shake the dust from your feet and leave."

And that was it. That was all Jesus told the twelve disciples who were going out on their own for the first time.

They did as Jesus said. No food, no clothes, no money, just a walking stick. They left towns that didn't welcome them. They stayed where people made them welcome and taught them to change their ways to follow God's ways. They healed many people. They could do this! They couldn't wait to tell Jesus!

Prayer: God of encouragement, as the disciples did what Jesus told them, we will try to live as Jesus taught. In Jesus' name, we pray. Amen.

The Ark Comes to Jerusalem
2 Samuel 6:1–5, 2b–19

King David, king of Judah and Israel! He moved from Hebron to Jerusalem, and all God's people were excited.

With God's help, David's army defeated the Philistines. Now David and all the people lived in peace in Jerusalem. It was time to bring the ark of the covenant, that special box that held the stone slabs with the Ten Commandments, to Jerusalem.

For many years, the ark of the covenant had been kept in safety at Abinadab's house. Finally, it would come to Jerusalem where the people could see it.

King David called for thirty thousand soldiers. Bringing the ark of the covenant to Jerusalem was an important job. When they got to Abinadab's house, the ark was loaded onto a cart, and off they went!

King David celebrated and praised God with songs, harps, stringed musical instruments, tambourines, and all kinds of rattles.

But something frightened David, and they left the ark of the covenant at Obededom's house. It stayed there for three months. During that time, God blessed Obededom's

midnight. They were in an upstairs room. It was crowded, and all the lamps made the room smoky. A teenager, Eutychus, was sitting in a window. He was very sleepy, and when he fell asleep he fell out the window and died. Paul hurried down the stairs. He hugged Eutychus. "It's okay," he said. "He's alive."

Everyone went back upstairs. Paul had something to eat, and then he taught the people until the sun came up. That morning Paul left. He planned not to stop in Ephesus. However, he sent for the leaders of the Ephesus church to meet him. He told them that he would never see them again and encouraged them to remember what he taught them and to remain faithful to Jesus the Christ. When it was time for Paul to leave, he and the church leaders prayed together. The church leaders from Ephesus hugged and kissed Paul. The thought of never seeing him again made them very sad.

Paul never returned to Ephesus, but he or one of his followers did write a letter to the church there. It is in the New Testament in the Bible, and it is called Ephesians.

Prayer: God of all, we are sad when friends leave us too, but we know that you are always with us. In Jesus' name, we pray. Amen.

(Sunday between July 17 and July 23 inclusive)

SEMICONTINUOUS

A House for God?
2 Samuel 7:1–14a

King David walked about his palace. It was a lovely home. Israel was at peace. Their enemies didn't bother them. Now what was he to do?

As he walked, he looked outside the palace. He could see the tent where the ark of the covenant sat. The ark of the covenant, that special box with the winged creatures with the Ten Commandments inside, was a symbol of God for the people of Israel. It reminded them that they belonged to God and that God was their God.

King David stopped and stared at the tent and the ark of the covenant. "Here I live in this beautiful palace, and the ark of the covenant sits under a tent. That can't be right!" he said to himself.

King David sent for the prophet Nathan. When Nathan came to him, the king said, "Look at me. I live in this beautiful palace. Look out there. God's ark of the covenant lives in a tent."

"Do what you are thinking," said Nathan. "God will be with you."

However, that night God came to Nathan. "My servant David wants to build a house for me. No. Tell him that he will not build a house for me. I don't want a house of wood or stone. I have always traveled with my people in a tent."

The next morning, Nathan went to King David. "My king," he said, "God spoke to me in the night. God said that you are not to build a house for the ark of the covenant. God said, 'I took you from the sheep's pasture and made you a shepherd of my people. I have stayed with you, no matter what. When you die, one of your sons will build a house for me.'"

King David was unhappy that he would not build the house for the ark of the covenant. He prayed to God, giving thanks for all that God had done for him and given to him and his family. King David was a faithful servant of God.

Prayer: God of the ages, you were with King David, and you are with us. Praise be to you. Amen.

❧ PROPER 11 ❧
(Sunday between July 17 and July 23 inclusive)

GOSPEL

Day after Day
Mark 6:30–34, 53–56

The disciples were excited to find Jesus. They had done what he told them to do. They went out in pairs to teach about Jesus and to heal people who were sick. They took no food, no extra clothes, and no money, just like Jesus told them. If a town didn't welcome them, they left. If a town welcomed them, they stayed. Now it was time to return to Jesus. Each pair of disciples was bubbling over with stories about what they had done.

When they found Jesus, each pair told him what they had done. But they were in a busy place. They couldn't even eat together there.

"Come on," said Jesus, "let's go to a quieter place where you can rest."

Jesus and the Twelve got into a boat and started off. But people saw them in the boat and saw where they were headed. The people hurried ahead of them. By the time Jesus and the disciples docked the boat, a large crowd was already there, waiting for them.

Jesus looked at the people. Deep down inside he felt what they were suffering. This feeling made him want to help them. So he sat down and taught the people many things about God and God's ways.

This happened again and again, on both sides of the Sea of Galilee. One day when they went by boat to Gennesaret, people immediately brought people to be healed. No matter where Jesus went, people found him. He went to cities, towns, villages, and out in the country. In every place, people asked to be healed. Jesus healed everyone who touched him.

Prayer: God of Compassion, just as Jesus saw suffering and helped the people, we will look into the eyes of people who are suffering and help them. In Jesus' name, we pray. Amen.

(Sunday between July 24 and July 30 inclusive)

One Lunch
John 6:1–21

Today's story about Jesus is so important that it is in all four Gospels: Matthew, Mark, Luke, and John. But only in the Gospel of John is a young person important in the story. Listen for how the youth is part of Jesus' miracle.

Jesus had been in Jerusalem where the Jewish leaders had given him a really hard time about working on the Sabbath day, a day that was honored as a day of rest and worship in the Ten Commandments.

To get some peace and quiet, away from the hassle of the crowds in Jerusalem for the Passover Feast, Jesus and the disciples crossed the Sea of Galilee to the other side.

But once again, a large crowd followed him. They had watched him heal people and wanted to be where he was. Jesus didn't stop to speak with the crowd. He just motioned to the disciples to come with him. They went up a mountain to a flat place, where Jesus sat down. His disciples sat with him.

When Jesus looked back in the direction that they had come, he saw all the people headed for him.

"Philip," Jesus said, "where can we buy food to feed this crowd of people coming toward us?" The question was to see if Philip could come up with a plan. Jesus already knew what he could do.

Philip looked at the crowd. What a lot of people! "It would take everything we earned in six months to buy food to feed all these people. And then each one would just get a little bit," said Philip. Of course, they were not even close to a place to buy food.

Andrew, Simon Peter's brother, was standing nearby and heard Jesus' question. He came over to Jesus with a young man, probably a teenager, and said, "He has five barley loaves and two fish. But that isn't much help to feed all these people."

Paying little attention to what Andrew said, Jesus said, "Have the people sit down on this nice grassy place." The disciples went among the crowd, telling the people, about five thousand of them, to sit down.

Jesus took a barley loaf from the young man. "Thank you for this food, God," he said. Then he started giving the five barley loaves and the two fish to the people. Amazingly, each person got enough to eat. Not too much, not too little, just enough.

When everyone had eaten, Jesus said to the disciples, "Gather up the leftover food. We don't want to waste anything."

The twelve disciples walked among the crowd sitting on the grass. Each one filled a basket with the leftover food. When the people saw the leftover food and realized that everyone had eaten, they saw that this was a sign, a miracle. They began to whisper to one another, "This man is surely a prophet of God come to the world."

Jesus could hear their whisperings and suspected that they were about to declare him a king. He did not want that to happen, so he went off by himself.

Prayer: God of plenty, this story of Jesus teaches us many things about your love for us. We praise you. In Jesus' name, we pray. Amen.

❧ PROPER 13 ❧
(Sunday between July 31 and August 6 inclusive)

Bread of Life
John 6:24–35

A fter Jesus fed that crowd of five thousand people and went off to be alone, he waited until evening came, and then he and the disciples crossed the Sea of Galilee to Capernaum.

The next day the crowd of people realized that a boat was missing and so were Jesus and the disciples. So some of them got into boats and sailed to Capernaum too.

They found Jesus there. "When did you get here?" they asked.

As was often the case, his response didn't answer their question. Jesus said, "You only came here to find me because I gave you food to eat yesterday. Don't be satisfied with food that you eat; look for what will satisfy your very being, deep inside you. That food will come from the one that God sends to you."

"What do we have to do to get that kind of food?" they asked.

"God only wants you to believe in the one whom God sends," was Jesus' answer.

"What will you do to make us believe?" they asked. "During the exodus, our ancestors ate manna in the desert."

"Yes, they did. And that food came from God, not Moses. Now God gives you the true bread from heaven."

"Give us that bread!" they exclaimed.

"I am the bread of life," said Jesus. "If you believe in me, you will never be hungry or thirsty."

I wonder what Jesus meant when he said that he was the bread of life. I wonder what the people thought.

Prayer: God of life, we will think about Jesus' words and pray that you will help us understand the "bread of life." In Jesus' name, we pray. Amen.

(Sunday between August 7 and August 13 inclusive)

COMPLEMENTARY

Elijah's Dilemma
1 Kings 19:4–8

God's prophet Elijah had just defeated one hundred prophets of the god Baal. Wouldn't you think he would be feeling pretty good? He wasn't, though, because Queen Jezebel, who worshiped Baal, was furious, and she was out to get Elijah. So Elijah ran away.

Elijah took his servant. They headed to Beersheba in Judah. Elijah told his servant to stay in Beersheba. Then Elijah walked in the wilderness desert all day, getting as far away from Queen Jezebel as he could. He took nothing with him.

As the sun began to set, Elijah found one broom bush. He sat under it, sad and scared.

"Enough, I've had enough," he cried to God. "Now, God, let me die. I am no better than those who came before me."

Elijah lay down under that one broom bush and went to sleep. An angel of God gently tapped him on the shoulder. "Get up, Elijah. Eat this cake and drink this water."

Elijah opened his eyes. Next to him on a hot stone was a cake, newly baked. Next to it was a jug of water. Elijah ate the cake and drank the water. Then he went back to sleep.

After a time, the angel was back. The angel tapped Elijah

gently on the shoulder. "Get up, Elijah. Eat and drink. If you don't, you won't be able to make this journey."

Elijah shook his head and got up. Again there was a freshly baked cake on a hot stone and a jug of water. Again he ate the cake and drank the water.

Feeling much stronger and better, Elijah walked for forty days and nights until he got to the mountain called Horeb, and he spent the night there.

Prayer: God of the prophets, you were with Elijah as he walked across the wilderness desert, and you are with us. Thank you. Amen.

(Sunday between August 7 and August 13 inclusive)

EPISTLE

Imitators of God
Ephesians 4:25–5:2

Y ou may remember that the apostle Paul, who traveled all over to begin churches, spent two years in Ephesus. He found some followers of Jesus there, so he stayed to help them begin a church.

When he could not return to Ephesus to see the people there, he did what Paul often did: he, or one of his followers, wrote a letter to the followers of Jesus in Ephesus. Paul must have heard that there were some troubles among the church members, because in his letter he tells them how to be faithful followers of Jesus and what not to do. Here is part of the letter:

> "Stop lying. Always tell the truth to one another because we are all sisters and brothers through Jesus the Christ. You are bound to get angry sometimes. But don't harm others with your anger, and get rid of it before the sun goes down. If you have taken things from others, stop it! Instead, work so you can help others.
>
> "Speak words that are good and that build up people and the community of the church. Don't say words

that hurt others. Be kind, caring toward others, and forgiving of everyone. Remember that God has forgiven us in Jesus the Christ.

"Imitate God just as you imitate those you love. Live and love. Follow the example of Jesus. Then you will be an imitator of God."

Just that little section from the letter had much for the people to think about. Which parts of it do you want to follow this week?

Prayer: God of love, we pray that we remember and live the way Paul told the people in the Ephesian church to live. In Jesus' name, we pray. Amen.

(Sunday between August 14 and August 20 inclusive)

SEMICONTINUOUS

King Solomon
1 Kings 2:10–12; 3:3–14

King David was old, and he died. God had promised David that his son would be the next king. It happened as God promised. David's son Solomon became the next king.

Solomon was firmly in place on the throne, but he had not yet talked with God. So King Solomon went to a shrine, a special place on a mountain where the king and the people offered sacrifices to God. They went there because the temple in Jerusalem had not been built yet.

King Solomon went to the shrine near Gibeon. During the night, he had a dream. God spoke to him in this dream.

"Solomon, ask me, what do you want from me?" said God.

"Lord God, you were kind to my father, David. His heart was always faithful. You kept your promise, and his son is now king of Israel. But, Lord God, I am young, and I don't know how to be a king over your people. They are so many that I can't count them. Please give me a listening heart, a discerning mind, so that I can tell good from evil and be a king who rules with justice."

"Good request," said God. "You did not ask for riches or a long life. I will give you a listening heart, a discerning mind. No king has ever been like you, and no one will be like you.

But because you did not ask for things for yourself, I will also give you riches and a long life, and everyone will hear about you. But I expect you to live in my ways as your father David did. If you do, all this will be yours."

King Solomon began to rule the people with a listening heart, a discerning mind. But will he remember to follow God's ways?

Prayer: God of wisdom, just as King Solomon did, we pray for a listening heart that we might be wise in all we say and do. Amen.

(Sunday between August 14 and August 20 inclusive)

EPISTLE

Worship Together
Ephesians 5:15–20

Imagine what it might have been like when followers of Jesus got together in a place far away from Jerusalem. They didn't have a church building, so they met in someone's house. They brought food to share with one another. They sang hymns and prayed. They talked about what it was to follow Jesus. Often these groups had heard about Jesus from Paul, who started many churches. But if they had questions or if they disagreed, they had no one to ask.

Sometimes Paul or other church leaders heard that things weren't going well so they wrote letters to those churches. Paul, or one of his followers, wrote to followers of Jesus in Ephesus. Although we don't know what he had heard, it seems that they may have forgotten the importance of worshiping God together. So Paul wrote:

> "Make wise decisions about what you do; don't be foolish. Be filled with God's spirit by singing hymns and psalms together. Make music to God in your hearts. Always give thanks to God for everything. Pray in the name of Jesus the Christ."

Be wise. Sing to God. Give thanks to God. This is how they were to be a people of God, a church. This is how we are to be a people of God too, the church today.

Prayer: God of Joy, our hearts are filled with music offered to you. We give thanks to you for everything, especially for our church. In Jesus' name, we pray. Amen.

(Sunday between August 21 and August 27 inclusive)

SEMICONTINUOUS

A House for God
1 Kings 8:(1, 6, 10–11), 22–30, 41–43

God told King David that he could not build a house for God, but God said that a son of David would build a house for God. Solomon was that son.

King Solomon, a man of great wisdom, knew that he was to build a house for God. King Hiram of Tyre, who was a friend of King David, agreed to help Solomon. All the finest woods and stones were used to build this house for God. It was three stories tall. A special place was set up for the ark of the covenant that still sat in a tent in Jerusalem. Gold was everywhere! Carvings of cherubim, or winged creatures, and palms decorated this house. It took seven years to build it, and it was the most beautiful building anyone had ever seen. And all the things inside, the lamps, the basins, everything was made of gold.

When all was ready, King Solomon brought into the house, for God, the donations of gold and silver from his father, King David.

Now it was time for the most important thing to be brought to the house for God: the ark of the covenant that held the stone slabs with the Ten Commandments, which God had given to Moses.

King Solomon told all the elders of Israel to come to Jerusalem. When they arrived, the priests brought the ark of the covenant from the tent and carried it to the house for God. They set it on the special place for it there.

King Solomon spread his hands before the presence of God and in front of the people. "O Lord God, who is above us and here with us, there is no other god like you." The people and King Solomon continued to worship God.

When they were finished, everyone feasted for fourteen days. Then everyone went home filled with joy.

Prayer: Holy God, you kept your promise to David that his son would build a house for you. By this we know that you will keep promises to us too. Amen.

A New Promise
Joshua 24:1–2a, 14–18

God chose Moses to lead the Israelites, the people of God, out of slavery in Egypt to a new home. It took them forty years to get there, and Moses died before they arrived. The new leader of the people was Joshua, also chosen by God. Now Joshua was very old, but he had one more thing to tell the people.

So Joshua called all the tribes of Israel to gather at Shechem. He reminded them of the stories of their ancestors, the generations before them. For example, Abraham and Sarah followed God's call. Their son Isaac was part of the promise from God. Isaac and Rebekah had two sons, Esau and Jacob. Esau and his family lived in the hill country, while Jacob and his family went to Egypt. When the Egyptians made the people slaves, God raised up Moses, Aaron, and Miriam, and they led them out of Egypt. God has always sent leaders to be with them.

The people nodded. They knew these stories well. They were important stories, family stories, God's stories. But now Joshua wanted to make sure the people in all twelve tribes of Israel were firmly and strongly with God.

"Respect God and serve God faithfully. Pay no attention to the gods of old. Choose today, right now, whether you will serve God or not. But I can tell you that for me and my family, we will serve God faithfully."

Immediately the people shouted, "We will serve God faithfully! We will serve no other gods! The Lord God brought us out of slavery in Egypt and stayed with us as we traveled. The Lord brought us to this land. We will serve God faithfully!"

Joshua made a covenant with the people. As a reminder of their promise, he took a huge stone and set it under the oak tree at Shechem. Joshua said to all the people, "See this stone. It will be a reminder to you that you have made this promise to serve God faithfully."

Then Joshua sent the people away. Now Joshua was one hundred and ten years old when he died. The people remembered their promise as long as the elders who knew Joshua were alive.

Prayer: God of Joshua and the twelve tribes of Israel, we have heard the promise the people made, and we will serve you faithfully too. Amen.

Unclean Hands
Mark 7:1–8, 14–15, 21–23

It was quite a scene when Jesus and the disciples landed at Gennesaret. As soon as Jesus got out of the boat, a crowd gathered, including people who were sick and wanted to be healed. Everyone who touched Jesus got better.

Then some Jewish religious experts and leaders came to Jesus. They had been watching the disciples eating food without washing their hands. Today, we wash our hands before we eat because we know about germs. In that day, they didn't know about germs, but they believed that they had to wash their hands to be holy before God.

"Why don't your disciples wash their hands as we have been taught?" the religious experts asked.

Jesus responded harshly. "You are hypocrites, you say one thing but you do something else. You talk about obeying God's laws, but your hearts are not settled in God's ways."

Then Jesus turned his back on these religious experts and looked at the crowd of people who were still surrounding him. He was still talking to the religious experts, but he was also teaching the crowd. "Listen, every one of you, it isn't the things that go into your body that make God sad. It is what comes out of you that makes God sad."

Later, when the disciples and Jesus were in a house alone, the disciples asked Jesus, "What did you mean about the things that come out of the body that make God sad?"

"It is the evil things that are in you that make God sad," said Jesus. "So when you do those things, you aren't following God's ways. Don't let your heart and mind want what other people have, and don't act as though you are better than other people. Don't say nasty things about other people."

I wonder what the crowd thought. And I wonder what the religious leaders were thinking. And I wonder how we are following Jesus.

Prayer: Holy God, we will try to keep Jesus' words in our hearts so that we remember to follow your ways. In Jesus' name, we pray. Amen.

(Sunday between September 4 and September 10 inclusive)

Listen, Jesus!
Mark 7:24–37

If today's story were written up in the newspaper, the head-line might be: Foreign Woman Confronts Jesus. This is what happened after Jesus and the disciples left Gennesaret and were in the area around the city of Tyre.

It seems that Jesus had gone to this region to get away from the crowds and get a bit of rest. He went into a house, but he didn't want anyone to know he was there. Fat chance of that!

A Greek woman, who was not Jewish, knew that Jesus had gone into this house. The woman's young daughter was sick. She came to the house and knelt down at Jesus' feet. She begged. "My daughter is sick. Heal her! Please!"

Jesus turned to look at the woman. He knew right away that she wasn't Jewish. "The children have to be fed first." Jesus believed that he first had to care for the Jewish peo-ple. But then he said, "You don't take the children's bread and throw it to the dogs."

The woman thought Jesus was calling her and anyone who wasn't Jewish a dog. But that didn't stop this Greek woman. Where other people might have hurried away, she stood right where she was. "Yes, but even the dogs under the table get the crumbs." Did she just remind Jesus that God was creator of all people, and she deserved help from him too?

Yes, I think she did, because Jesus thought for a moment and said, "Good answer. You are right. Go home to your daughter. She is well."

Not waiting for another word from Jesus, the woman ran home. Yes, her daughter was in her bed, but she was well!

Prayer: God of all people, teach us every day that you are the God of each and every person. In Jesus' name, we pray. Amen.

(Sunday between September 11 and September 17 inclusive)

Hard Words to Hear
Mark 8:27–38

Jesus and the disciples were still on the move. Now they were going into villages around Caesarea Philippi. Jesus took the opportunity to teach the disciples as they walked together. On this day Jesus used a question to begin the conversation.

"Who do people say that I am?" he asked them.

"Some say you are John the baptizer."

"I've heard people say you are Elijah."

"Many people think you are one of God's prophets."

Then Jesus got to the point. "But who do you say that I am?"

Without skipping a beat, Peter said, "You are the Christ, the Messiah, the one sent from God."

But Jesus didn't smile and say to Peter, "Good job. You are right! I'm proud of you."

No, Jesus said to Peter and all the other disciples, "Don't tell anyone what Peter has just said. Do not tell them that I am the Christ."

I wonder why Jesus didn't want them to tell anyone this exciting news. Could it be that people, especially the religious leaders, weren't ready to hear that Jesus was the Christ?

Prayer: Loving God, we know that Jesus is the Christ, the one you sent to us. Give us the courage to tell people about him. In Jesus' name, we pray. Amen.

(Sunday between September 18 and September 24 inclusive)

See This Child
Mark 9:30–37

Jesus was trying to keep away from crowds of people who wanted him to teach and to heal them. He needed time alone with his disciples. He had much to tell them. The closer they got to Jerusalem, the more important it was to teach them.

Sometimes as they walked, the disciples talked among themselves. This happened as they came close to Capernaum. And from their voices, it sounded like they were arguing. So when they got to a seaside town and went into a house, Jesus asked them, "What were you talking about on the road just now?"

No one said a word. No one looked at Jesus. Jesus waited. He didn't ask his question again. He just waited.

You see, they had been arguing about which one of them was the best, the greatest. Each disciple knew Jesus did not want to hear that.

But Jesus knew what they had been saying. As their voices got more excited, even angry, he could hear what they were saying. No one had to tell Jesus the answer to his question.

Jesus sat down. This was a signal that he wanted them to listen to what he had to say. In that day, teachers sat down to teach their students.

The disciples gathered around him, ready to listen. Each one felt a little ashamed that they had been arguing about who was the greatest.

"Listen to me," Jesus began. "If you want to be best or great, you have to be willing to be last and to help anyone who needs help. You have to be ready to be the least powerful of everyone."

Then Jesus did something surprising. He called a child standing nearby to come to him. He stood the child in front of him where the disciples could see the child. He put his arms around the child and said, "When you welcome a child like this in my name, you are welcoming me. When you welcome me like this, you are welcoming the one who sent me, God."

The disciples looked at Jesus. Who worries about welcoming a child? Children were the least important of all people. What was Jesus telling them?

Prayer: Loving God, whether we are big or small, we can welcome all people in your name. We will also try to help anyone who needs help. In Jesus' name, we pray. Amen.

❧ PROPER 21 ❦
(Sunday between September 25 and October 1 inclusive)

Saltiness
Mark 9:38–50*

Jesus kept the child by his side. He hoped seeing the child had helped the disciples understand that they were to serve and help everyone, especially people who didn't seem to be important.

Everyone was quiet. Then John said, "Jesus, we saw a man healing people in your name. But this man has not been traveling with us. We didn't know him, and we told him to stop."

"Don't stop him," said Jesus. "If he was able to heal in my name, then he is on our side. If he is on our side, he won't be against us. If someone gives you a cup of water because you are with me, that person will be rewarded."

Then Jesus pointed to the child at his side. "If you, or anyone else, does something to cause a child like this to forget God, you will be in big trouble with God. Don't do anything that will separate you from God. What you do should keep you enclosed in God's love and among God's people."

The disciples looked at one another. Sometimes Jesus' words were hard to understand. Were they doing something

---

*A story about Esther, the Old Testament lection for Proper 21, can be found on page 150 of Stories for Special Sundays.

that would separate them from God? Why would they do something to cause a child to forget God?

Jesus continued, "You should be like salt. Salt has many uses. We use it to add flavor to our food. We use it to preserve food. Sometimes a worker is paid in salt. But if salt has lost its saltiness, what good is it? Keep your saltiness. Be at peace with one another."

Be like salt, and be at peace. What does that mean for Jesus' followers today?

Prayer: Mighty God, as we try to understand Jesus' words, send your Spirit to us to help our understanding. In Jesus' name, we pray. Amen.

Let Them Come
Mark 10:2–16

Everywhere Jesus went, Jewish religious leaders watched and listened. It was no different on this day. Jesus and the disciples left Capernaum and went to the area of Judea. Here too, crowds had heard about him and showed up everywhere he went. And time after time the Jewish religious leaders tried to catch him in saying something wrong by asking him questions. Sometimes Jesus answered with a story, and other times he asked them a question.

Usually the people who came wanted to hear Jesus teach about God. Or they brought friends and family members who were sick for Jesus to heal them. But on this day, something else was happening too.

Parents holding their children's hands or carrying younger children came to Jesus. They wanted Jesus to bless their children, to touch them and give them God's blessing.

Jesus had just been dealing with those pesky Jewish religious leaders, always asking questions. The disciples thought Jesus looked tired. So they stepped in front of the parents with their children.

"Don't bother Jesus," they said in a way that sounded like

they were scolding. "He is tired. He needs some time alone. Go away. Come back later."

Jesus heard his disciples sending the families away. Jesus wasn't just annoyed at this; Jesus was angry.

"Don't send those people away!" he shouted at his disciples. "Let the children come to me. You, you will need to be like these children if you want to be in God's kingdom. If you don't welcome children like these, you won't be right with God."

Then Jesus hugged and blessed each child, giving them God's love.

I wonder how the disciples looked as they watched Jesus and the children.

Prayer: God of love, whether we are children or adults, we want your love and your blessing. In Jesus' name, we pray. Amen.

❦ PROPER 23 ❦

(Sunday between October 9 and October 15 inclusive)

Another Question for Jesus
Mark 10:17–31

Jesus and the disciples were walking along the road when a man came running to catch up with Jesus. He clearly wanted to speak to Jesus. He had an important question to ask him. Now he wasn't one of the Jewish religious leaders, so he wasn't trying to trick Jesus.

Panting, he asked, "Good teacher, what must I do to live forever with God?"

"Why do you call me 'good'?" asked Jesus. "Only God is good." That sounded just a bit unfriendly, but Jesus continued. "Obey God's commandments. Don't murder. Don't steal. Honor your mother and father."

"Teacher," the man interrupted, "I have done that since I was a child. What more can I do?"

Now this man had Jesus' full attention. Jesus looked at the man with love and concern.

"Well, there is something more you can do. Sell everything you have and give the money to the poorest people you can find. Then, come back to me and go with me. If you do this, you will have more than followed God's commandments."

The man looked sad because he had a lot of stuff. It says in the Bible that the man went away. Then Jesus turned to his disciples and said, "It is very hard for rich people, for people with lots of stuff, to live with God forever."

Now I wonder if the man looked sad because he knew he couldn't sell all this stuff, or if he looked sad because he knew he had to sell all his stuff and how hard that would be. What do you think?

Prayer: God of the poor, whether we think we have a lot of stuff or not, we know that there are other people who are in need. Help us to help them. In Jesus' name, we pray. Amen.

❧ PROPER 24 ❦
(Sunday between October 16 and October 22 inclusive)

Me, Choose Me
Mark 10:35–45

After the man who had a lot of stuff left, Jesus and the disciples continued on the road to Jerusalem. Jesus was quiet. Perhaps he was thinking about the man who asked how he could live with God forever, wondering if the man would return to travel with him.

But the disciples were chatting as they walked along. Maybe they were wondering about the man too. Perhaps some were thinking about the children that Jesus blessed earlier. Others may have been thinking about where they would spend the night and where they would get food.

As they walked along, James and John, the sons of Zebedee, caught up with Jesus. James and John, along with Simon Peter and Andrew, were the first people Jesus asked to follow him and be his disciples. They had been with Jesus from the beginning.

"Jesus," they said.

"Yes, what is it?" asked Jesus.

"Promise that you will do anything that we ask you."

Surely Jesus looked at them with arched eyebrows. What kind of request is this? Why did they think Jesus would make that promise to them?

But Jesus was curious and asked, "What do you want me to do for you?"

"When you are king, let one of us sit on your right and the other sit on your left." These were the most important seats. People knew you were special if you sat on either side of the king.

Jesus could hardly believe what they were asking. "Do you think you can take what will happen to me? You have no idea what you are asking."

But that didn't stop James and John. "We can, of course," they both answered.

Looking at the brothers sadly, Jesus said, "Who will sit at my right and my left is not for me to decide."

When the other disciples heard about this conversation, they were angry at James and John.

Jesus took this moment to teach his disciples one more time about what it was to lead God's people. "If you follow me, you won't look for ways to show how special you are. You will look for ways to serve, to care for people, all people."

It seems that the disciples had a hard time learning about leadership from Jesus.

Prayer: Creator God, help us understand leadership as Jesus taught and lived it. In Jesus' name, we pray. Amen.

❧ PROPER 25 ❧
(Sunday between October 23 and October 29 inclusive)

Blind Bartimaeus
Mark 10:46–52

Jesus and the disciples had just walked through Jericho, which was about twenty miles from the city of Jerusalem.

As they were leaving Jericho, a crowd followed Jesus and the disciples. Their noise attracted the attention of Bartimaeus, who was blind and sat by the side of this road every day. He sat there hoping that people would give him money or food. Being blind, he had no way to work.

He could hear people talking as they walked along the road in front of Jesus.

"Did you see the way he took care of those questions from the religious leaders?"

"And what about the way he hugged and blessed the children?"

"This Jesus is amazing."

"Yes, Jesus heals and teaches with a power I've never seen before."

"I've heard that he is from Nazareth, and his father Joseph is from the family of David."

Hearing all this, Bartimaeus called, "Jesus, son of David, heal me!"

"Quiet," scolded some of the people passing by. "Stop shouting."

But that made Bartimaeus shout even louder, "Jesus, son of David, heal me!"

When Jesus heard Bartimaeus, he said to those around him, "Bring that man who was shouting to me."

The same people who were telling Bartimaeus to be quiet now said, "Jesus is calling for you. Get up, get up!"

Bartimaeus tossed his coat to the ground and stood up. The crowd pushed him in Jesus' direction.

"What do you want me to do?" asked Jesus.

"Teacher, I want to see," said Bartimaeus.

"You are healed," said Jesus.

At that very minute, Bartimaeus could see. And he followed Jesus on the road to Jerusalem.

Prayer: God of healing, may our eyes be opened to see Jesus too, and may that give us the courage to follow him. In Jesus' name, we pray. Amen.

Ruth and Naomi
Ruth 1:1–18

In the ancient town of Bethlehem, long before Jesus was born, food was hard to get. No rain, no plants. Elimelech and Naomi, with their sons Mahlon and Chillion, moved to the foreign land of Moab. The decision was hard because Moab was a land of enemies of the Israelites; the decision was easy because there was plenty of food there. They settled in, and their sons married Moabite women, Orpah and Ruth.

Then Elimelech died, leaving Naomi alone in a foreign land, except for her two sons. Then her sons died. That left three widows—Naomi, Ruth, and Orpah—on their own. Not a good thing in those days—widows with no male relatives to protect them.

When Naomi heard that the drought was over and plants were growing again in Bethlehem, she decided to return to her homeland. She urged Ruth and Orpah to return to the homes of their mothers in Moab.

Both women refused. "Look," said Naomi, "even if I had sons now, would you want to wait until they were men to marry them? No, go to your mothers." Eventually Orpah agreed to do what Naomi wanted, but Ruth refused.

"No matter what," said Ruth, "I will go where you go. I will live where you live. Your people will be my people. Your God will be my God. I will be buried where you are buried. Nothing, not even death, will keep me away from you."

Naomi could see it was no use to argue with Ruth, so the two widows set off for Bethlehem. The people were surprised to see Naomi and especially surprised to see the Moabite woman with her.

As they saw how much Ruth loved Naomi, they forgot that she was a Moabite. One of the men noticed Ruth, and eventually they were married. They had a son, Obed. Naomi was the happiest grandmother in Bethlehem! Obed grew up and had a son named Jesse, who had a son named David who became king of all Israel.

Prayer: God of all nations, we marvel at the great love and care that Ruth had for Naomi. That loving-kindness reminds us of your love for us. Amen.

Hear, O Israel
Deuteronomy 6:1–9

"Hear, O Israel!" These three words begin the most important commandment from God. It's found in the book of Deuteronomy, chapter 6, in the Bible. These words introduce instructions Moses received from God for the people of Israel, God's people.

The Israelites were close to moving into the land that God promised would be their new home after slavery in Egypt and all those years of wandering through the desert wilderness. People were excited that the journey was almost over, but God wanted to be sure that they had their heads and hearts in the right place. God gave lots, really lots, chapters full, of instructions for Moses to tell to the people.

Moses said, "Listen to these words, Israel. Everyone, adults and children, listen carefully. Follow God's words carefully so you will continue to grow and do well in this new land of milk and honey."

Then Moses paused, to make certain that everyone was listening. When the murmuring stopped and only the sounds of nature could be heard, Moses said, "Israel, listen! Our God is the LORD! The only God!"

Moses paused again, and some of the older people remembered the time they had made a golden calf and worshiped it. No, God is the only God.

"Love God with all your heart, with all your being, and with all your strength!" said Moses. "Keep these words always in your minds. Say them to your children. Talk about them when you are at home together and when you are away from home. Recall them as the last thing you think of before you go to sleep and the first thing when you wake up. Keep them on the doorframe of your home."

Even to this day, Jewish families place a box on their doorframe with this commandment and these words. The box is called a *mezuzah*. These words are called the *Shema*. The word "listen" is *shema* in Hebrew.

Jesus said this command to love God with all your heart, being, and strength was the most important commandment of all. These ancient words are for us to remember too: Love God with all your heart, with all your being, and with all your strength.

Prayer: God of all, as Moses told the people and Jesus taught the people, we will love God with all our heart, with all our being, and with all our strength. Amen.

A Widow Helps Elijah
1 Kings 17:8–16

Things were really bad in Israel. No rain, and the rivers and brooks were drying up. Queen Jezebel was out to get God's prophet Elijah. Elijah was on the run.

Elijah was hiding out near the Jordan River when God's word came to him. "Go to the town of Zarephath near Sidon, which is where Jezebel is from. I have put it into the heart of a woman there, a widow, to take care of you."

Elijah set off for Zarephath. When he walked inside the town gate, he saw a woman dressed in widow's clothing gathering sticks. He called to her, "Please get me some water in this cup. I'm thirsty."

It was the rule of the land to offer water to a traveler, so the woman started off to get a drink of water for Elijah. He called after her. "And bring me a piece of bread."

The woman turned around. Water she could get for him, but not a piece of bread, for she had none.

"As sure as your God lives, I have only a little meal and a little oil to bake bread," she said. "I am gathering these sticks to make a fire to use that bit of meal and oil to bake bread for my son and me. Then we will starve."

"Don't worry," said Elijah. "Make a small piece of bread for me. Then make some for you and your son. For your jar of meal and your jug of oil will never be empty until it rains again. God, the God of Israel, told me this."

The widow did what Elijah told her. Indeed, her jar of meal and her jug of oil were never empty. It was just as God had told Elijah.

Prayer: God of enough, the widow had faith in the God of Elijah. May we have faith in you too. Amen.

(Sunday between November 6 and November 12 inclusive)

GOSPEL

A Faithful Offering
Mark 12:38–44

Jesus answered wisely all the questions people asked him, so no one dared to ask another question. He continued to teach in the temple. Many people came to hear him, including the same religious leaders who had been questioning him.

Knowing they were listening, Jesus told the crowd, "Watch out for those religious leaders who want to show you how important they are. They wear long, fancy robes to show off. They strut around so everyone will know they are important. They expect you to bow to them in the marketplace. They expect you to step aside as they walk by. They want the seats and places in the synagogue and at feasts that will let everyone know they are the most important people in the room. But they are also the ones who say long prayers to make you think they are the holiest of people, even as they cheat widows, making them homeless. One day they will be judged."

After saying this, Jesus and the disciples left. They stopped across from the collection box for the temple. Jesus and the disciples watched the people come and go.

Many people dressed in fine clothes, who were obviously rich, dropped lots of money in the collection box. When they gave their money, it clanged and banged, making a loud noise to attract people's attention.

Then Jesus watched a widow, who looked poor from the sight of her clothes. She walked to the collection box and carefully dropped one, two small coins into it. They hardly made a sound. She quietly walked away.

"Did you see that widow?" Jesus asked the disciples. "She is the most faithful person I have seen put money in the collection box while we have been standing here. She gave only two small coins, but that was all the money she had. Those rich people who dropped in lots of money and made lots of noise, they gave only some spare change that they really didn't need. The widow loved God so much that she gave money that she needed for food."

Wasn't that something for the disciples to think about? Two small coins were a sign of more faithfulness than the handfuls of coins from the rich people.

Prayer: Loving God, show us the way to be faithful to you whether we can give two coins or many coins. Amen.

A Prayer and a Promise
1 Samuel 1:4–20

Perhaps you know the story of the boy Samuel who lived at the temple where Eli was the priest. God called to Samuel in the night and had a message for Eli. If you wondered why Samuel lived at the temple and not with his parents, Hannah and Elkanah, in Ephraim, this story tells you how that came to be.

Hannah wanted a baby so much. Elkanah's other wife, Penninah, had children, but Hannah did not. Every year when it was time to go to worship God at the holy place in Shiloh, Hannah prayed for a baby. Penninah made fun of Hannah and teased her. "Still no baby, Hannah? Guess God isn't as pleased with you as God is with me," she taunted. This always made Hannah cry and so sad that she didn't eat.

Elkanah tried to make Hannah feel better. "Please eat. Please don't cry. Am I not as important to you as ten babies?"

But Hannah just sobbed.

On this trip to Shiloh to worship God, Hannah went to the place of prayer to sit before God. She walked past Eli, who was sitting at the entrance. She knelt and prayed, moving her lips but not speaking aloud. She cried as she prayed to God. "God, look at me. I am so sad and upset that I have no babies. Please remember me! Give me a baby boy! If you do, I will give him back to serve you for his whole life."

Eli watched all this. He thought she was drunk on wine.

"Woman," said Eli, "how long are you going to act like a drunk?"

"Sir," said Hannah, "I am not drunk; I am a very sad woman. I have been praying with all my energy to God. I haven't had anything to drink."

"Go in peace," said Eli. "May God give you what you want so much."

After that Hannah and Elkanah had a son, whom they named Samuel. Hannah kept her promise to God. When Samuel was still a young boy she took him to Shiloh to live and work with Eli.

And that is why Samuel grew up in the holy place in Shiloh with Eli.

Prayer: God of wonders, the amazing thing is that you hear our prayers and answer them in your own way. Amen.

Trust in God
Psalm 16

Can we praise God for creation? Can we yell at God when bad things happen? Can we thank God for God's faithfulness? Can we complain to God that God is not paying attention? Can we ask God to help or protect us? Yes, we can do all these things as the people who wrote the psalms in the Old Testament did. And sometimes they did more than one of these things in the same psalm.

Psalm 16, the psalm for today, begins with asking for God's help. Listen:

> "God, protect me. You are my safe place.
>   God, you are my God.
>   I am nothing without you."

When we want to remember that we are in God's hands and need God's protection, the beginning of Psalm 16 is good to remember.

The psalm continues with words to help us remember what we know about God from the past, our heritage. Listen again:

"God, you control everything about me,
   and that is good.
"You have always been with me,
   at my right hand,
   and I will not fall down."

The writer of this psalm has known good things about God from the past. So the psalm ends with words that we can be sure that God will continue to be present, no matter what.

"When I remember this,
   I am filled with joy
   And every inch of my body relaxes.
"You will never leave me, your faithful follower."

These words were written thousands and thousands of years ago. But they are words that we can read and say today, and be filled with joy.

Prayer: Our God, whom we trust, we are filled with joy knowing that you are with us no matter what. Amen.

A Wondrous Vision
Revelation 1:4b–8

Have you ever wondered what it would be like to live on an island all by yourself? Well, I don't know if a man named John was all by himself, and he probably wasn't. But John had to live on the island of Patmos, away from other Christians. It seems that John had gotten into trouble for preaching about Jesus and God. While he was on the island, he had some amazing visions from God.

John wrote down these visions so other Christians could read them and get hope from them. Some were about riders on fiery horses with warnings for the people in the cities of Asia. Some were comforting and full of hope, as when he described a new heaven and a new earth where there was no sadness, no crying at all. But all of the visions were from God, and that is how John begins the book of the Bible called Revelation.

> "John, to the seven churches in Asia.
> "Grace and peace to you from the one who is,
> who was, and is to come
> and from Jesus Christ, the ruler of the kings of
> the earth.

"All glory be to God who loves us and brought us
          together to be a people
     to serve Jesus Christ and God. All glory be
          forever and ever! Amen.
"Look, Jesus is coming on a cloud
     and everyone will see him,
     even the people who didn't believe him.
"God says, 'I am the Alpha and the Omega, the
          beginning and the end.
     I am who is, who was, and who is to come,
          the Almighty.'"

Such powerful words in John's vision. Such powerful
words for us to remember about Jesus and God.

Prayer: Almighty God, we are amazed at your power and
your glory. We praise you today and forever. Amen.

STORIES FOR SPECIAL SUNDAYS

Baptize Them
Matthew 28:16–20

Why do we baptize babies, and sometimes older children and adults? Perhaps it's because Jesus was baptized, and we follow his example. But perhaps it's because Jesus told the disciples to baptize people. This is how it happened.

Before Jesus died and came back to life in the resurrection, he sent his disciples in pairs to other towns to heal people just like Jesus did. Jesus gave them the power to do this, but he didn't tell them to baptize the people. Remember how he told them not to take extra clothes or food, but to rely on the hospitality, or welcome, of people? Remember how excited they were when they returned to tell Jesus what they had done?

That was great, but it wasn't until after the resurrection that Jesus told them to teach and baptize. Jesus told the women who came to the tomb to tell the disciples that he would see them again in Galilee.

And he did. The eleven disciples went to Galilee to the mountain where he told them to go. Sure enough, Jesus was there. The disciples fell to their knees to worship Jesus. But some still weren't sure that what they saw was real.

Still, Jesus told them, "I have all power over heaven and earth. You are to go to all nations. Baptize them in the name of the Father, in the name of the Son, and in the name of the Holy Spirit. Teach them everything that I have taught you. And I will be with you every day."

That is why we baptize people and teach them all that we know about Jesus and what he taught. We baptize them, and this morning we will baptize (*name of person*) in the name of the Father, and of the Son, and of the Holy Spirit.

Prayer: God of the Trinity, may we keep our promise to (*name of person*) to teach (*her/him*) everything we know about you and Jesus and all that he taught. Amen.

A New Queen*
Esther

King Ahasuerus had gotten rid of the queen. He needed a new queen, so he had a beauty contest. The winner was a beautiful young Jewish woman, Esther, but she didn't tell anyone that she was Jewish. Remember that.

Haman, a high official of the king, had the king decree that everyone was to bow down to Haman when he walked by. Everyone did except Mordecai, a relative of Esther. Mordecai, being a Jew, believed that you only bowed down to God. This made Haman so angry that he began to plot ways to kill not just Mordecai but all the Jews. He convinced the king to send out a decree that anyone who did not follow all the king's laws was to die.

When Mordecai heard this, he got word to Esther that all Jews, her people, were in great trouble. But Esther sent word to Mordecai that there was nothing she could do. She couldn't even talk to the king unless he sent for her. Finally, Mordecai sent this message to Esther: "Don't think that you are not in danger because you live in the palace. If you don't speak up, we will all die. Who knows? Perhaps it was for this very moment that you came to live in the palace."

*The story of Queen Vashti is on page xxv of the introduction. This story is the Old Testament lection for Year B, Proper 21, semicontinuous stream (Esther 7:1–6, 9–10; 9:20–22).

Now Esther understood how terrible all this was. She invited the king and Haman to dinner, two times. After the first dinner, King Ahasuerus couldn't sleep, so he began to read about what had happened since he had become king. He read about a time that Mordecai saved his life. The next day he asked Haman, "What could I do for someone I really want to honor?"

Haman, thinking the king was going to honor him, said, "Give the man one of your royal robes and one of your horses. Lead him through the streets. He should shout, 'This is what the king does for someone he wants to honor.'"

So the king told Haman to do this for Mordecai. The look on Haman's face was sour.

That evening, Esther invited the king and Haman for the second dinner. At it, the king said, "What is your wish, Queen Esther? What can I do for you?"

"If the king wishes," said Esther, "give me my life and the lives of my people. We are to be killed."

"Who has done this?" demanded the king.

When Esther pointed to Haman and said, "This evil one, this hater," the king was so angry he left.

King Ahasuerus ordered that Haman be killed, but he could not undo the decree to kill the Jews. Instead, an order went out that the Jews would be able to defend themselves. And Mordecai now lived in Haman's house and was the official most important to the king.

To this day, Jews celebrate Esther's brave acts at the festival of Purim. They tell the story and celebrate. They also give gifts of food and money to people who are poor.

Prayer: Almighty God, you placed Esther in the palace where she could help her people. Make us aware of how we can help others where we are. Amen.

Set Free
Exodus 12

L ife as slaves in Egypt was terrible! Pharaoh wouldn't even give them time off to worship God. So when God told Moses to free the Israelite slaves, they were excited. The way that happened is remembered with the celebration of Passover every year.

When Moses demanded that Pharaoh let the Israelite slaves go free, Pharaoh refused, time and time again. God sent disasters—the Nile River turned to blood, frogs showed up everywhere, lice covered all the people and animals, insects swarmed over the whole land, skin sores broke out on people and animals, thunder and hail destroyed every plant, locusts covered the land—and nothing would change Pharaoh's mind. Finally, God had enough.

God gave these instructions to Moses for the Israelites, "Kill a lamb. Take some of the lamb's blood and smear it on the doorframe of your house. Roast the lamb and eat it with your family. Eat all of it or burn what is not eaten. When you eat, wear your clothes and your sandals and have a walking stick nearby so you can leave quickly. God will pass over the land, and the oldest child and animal in every family will die.

But the oldest children in your families will not die because your house will be marked with the blood of the lamb."

When Moses told this to the people, they surely looked at one another. Was this really true? What would happen to them?

"And every year, in this first month, we will celebrate this Passover by God with unleavened flat bread and bitter herbs to remember how God saved us," Moses told the people. "And when your children ask why we do this, you will tell them the story of how God saved us, and you will praise God together."

Even today, Jewish families and friends gather to celebrate a meal together and to tell the story of the Passover, remembering it as their story too.

Prayer: God of the Passover, your ways are beyond our understanding, and we praise you along with our Jewish neighbors for the ways that you free them and us even today. Amen.

God's Faithful Love
Psalm 136

The roads to Jerusalem were crowded. God's people were coming to celebrate God and give thanks to God. They came three times each year, if they were able. They came at the end of the harvest for the festival of Booths, when they brought grain from their fields. They came for Passover, when they remembered the exodus after being slaves in Egypt. They came for the festival of weeks, the day we call Pentecost. For them it was fifty days after Passover. For us, it is fifty days after Easter.

So many years ago, they traveled to Jerusalem on foot or maybe a donkey. They sang praises to God as they traveled, songs that helped them remember all that God had done for them. They sang hymns that thanked God. Some of those songs are in the book of Psalms in our Bible. We don't know the melodies, but we have the words to one-hundred-fifty hymns and prayers to God.

A few of those psalms are called "psalms of ascent" or "pilgrimage psalms." *Ascent* refers to the people walking *up* to the city of Jerusalem. *Pilgrimage* refers to the fact that these trips to Jerusalem were part of being faithful to God and God's commandments.

Here are some verses from one of the pilgrimage psalms. When I hold up my hand, everyone say: "God's faithful love lasts forever." (*Practice the line two or three times.*)

> "Give thanks to the Lord
>   because he is good.
>   **God's faithful love lasts forever.**
> "Give thanks to the only one
>   who makes great wonders—
>   **God's faithful love lasts forever.**
> "Give thanks to the one
>   who made the skies with skill—
>   **God's faithful love lasts forever.**
> "Give thanks to the one
>   who shaped the earth on the water—
>   **God's faithful love lasts forever.**
> "Give thanks to the one
>   who made the great lights—
>   **God's faithful love lasts forever.**
> "The sun to rule the day—
>   **God's faithful love lasts forever.**
> "The moon and stars
>   to rule the night—
>   **God's faithful love lasts forever.**
> "Give thanks to the God of heaven—
>   **God's faithful love lasts forever."**

Prayer: All thanks to you, God, for your faithful love that lasts forever. Amen and amen.

Index

NOTE: Entries show the volume and Sunday of stories in the series, *Feasting on the Word Children's Sermons*. Entries in parenthesis indicate other appearances of the lection in the Revised Common Lectionary where the story may also be used.

❧ LECTIONARY DATES ❦

❧ STORIES FOR SPECIAL SUNDAYS ❦

CPSIA information can be obtained
at www.ICGtesting.com
Printed in the USA
BVOW03s1256011017
496345BV00002B/78/P